the salad book

Michele Evans

HENRY REGNERY COMPANY · CHICAGO

Library of Congress Cataloging in Publication Data

Evans, Michele.
  The salad book.

  1. Salads. I. Title.
TX807.E88   641.8′3   74-34003
ISBN 0-8092-8301-8

To Maureen Baron

Copyright © 1975 by Michele Evans. All rights reserved.
Published by Henry Regnery Company
180 North Michigan Avenue, Chicago, Illinois 60601
Manufactured in the United States of America
Library of Congress Catalog Card Number: 74-34003
International Standard Book Number: 0-8092-8301-8

Published simultaneously in Canada by
Fitzhenry & Whiteside Limited
150 Lesmill Road
Don Mills, Ontario M3B 2T5
Canada

According to a Spanish proverb,

> Four persons are wanted to make a salad:
> A spendthrift for oil,
> A miser for vinegar,
> A counsellor for salt,
> And a madman to stir it all up.

Contents

Introduction

Larousse Gastronomique defines salads as: "Dishes made up of herbs, plants, vegetables, eggs, meat and fish, seasoned with oil, vinegar, salt and pepper, with or without any other ingredients."

Today salad ingredients may be almost any edible—cheese, pasta, rice, fruit, bean sprouts, and even lotus roots, as you will discover later in the book.

No one knows how or when people invented salads, but primitive people undoubtedly knew the taste of greens and herbs. The word *salad* comes from the Latin word *sal,* meaning "salt," and was probably derived from the Roman custom of eating greens with salt.

Salads have gained and lost popularity more often than any other category of foods. Since the turn of the century, they have had a reputation as a ladies' luncheon food or a side dish for a broiled steak and baked potato. With the rising interest in health foods, salads are now enjoying great popularity because of their value as a health food. It is a reputation well deserved —it is almost impossible to make an unhealthy salad.

The art of saladmaking is easily mastered, whether you are planning to tackle an elaborate main-dish salad or to prepare a simple but supreme green salad with vinaigrette.

Ingredients for salads should always be the freshest and the best available, because generally they are used raw. It is fortunate that many salad materials are seasonal—they are at their best when their prices are lowest.

Dressings are as important to a salad as the other ingredients. The oil must always be fresh, as should be the mayonnaise, cream, and vinegar. Many people keep a variety of oils for use in dressings. You may even want to mix several kinds of oils to obtain a taste that you particularly enjoy. Lemon juice, preferably fresh, too, is an interesting substitute for vinegar on occasion.

Learning to plan the right salad for a meal is a skill in itself. If the salad is served as a side dish, it should balance the main dish. If you are serving a heavily spiced meat, for example, you will probably want it accompanied by a green salad with a simple vinaigrette. For a meal featuring a simple roast, you might want a more elaborate tossed salad, or a green salad with a spicier dressing. Hearty salads, such as those containing pasta, rice, or potatoes, are often served as side dishes. You might also include a simple tossed or green salad in the meal. Tomato salads go with many foods, but they generally do not go with a meal that has another dish with tomatoes in it.

Meals at which salads star are even less of a problem, because you plan the menu around the salad. Sample menus beginning on page 143 will help you plan meals around salads.

Presentation is one of the more important aspects of saladmaking. Salads—simple or elaborate—should always be pleasing to the eye and add color to a meal. Use garnishes creatively to add color, but do not overdo it. Anything too manufactured does not look as if it wants to be eaten.

A good rule of thumb is to use real foods for garnish. Consider the possibilities of using this list of garnishes, all of which are natural:

thin slices of red onion, separated into rings
radish roses
cubes of cheese or grated cheese
eggs, hard-boiled and cut into rings, or grated and sprinkled over a salad (grate the yolks and whites separately and sprinkle in alternate swirls)
stuffed olives
herbs and spices
  chopped chives
  parsley
  paprika
  celery seeds
  fennel seeds
capers
nuts
pimiento strips
anchovy fillets
croutons
toast rounds or triangles
pepper
  black, crushed
  green peppercorns

Tastes in salads vary from country to country, depending upon the climate and traditions of the people. Northern Europeans use a great deal of fresh and dried fish, meat, and potatoes in salads, perhaps because their climate prohibits the growth of plentiful quantities of vegetables. People in tropical countries make excellent use of the lovely and varied fruits that are available to them. Americans are known for their creative molded salads and colorful tossed salads. The French generally prefer a green salad with vinaigrette, except those who live in the southern regions, where the salads become as colorful and flavorful as those of nearby Italy and Spain.

The French also prefer to eat their salads after the main course, a custom that is growing in popularity in the United States. A salad is particularly refreshing after a hearty meal and seems to prepare the palate for the next course, be it a simple cheese with fruit or an elaborate dessert.

The great number of recipes in this book are meant only to get you started. Unlike other food categories that require specific amounts of ingredients for the success of a recipe, salads can be made in endless combinations with a variety of ingredients.

I hope that you will enjoy this collection of recipes, but even more, I hope that you will discover the joys of creating your own salads.

Michele Evans

Salad Utensils and Equipment

The following equipment and utensils are important in the preparation of salads. There are many other devices that are helpful, but these are the essentials for successful saladmaking.

chopping block   Board made of heavy wood used for all kinds of chopping in saladmaking. It is advisable also to have a small wooden chopping board to use just for garlic and onion, because their strong flavor stays on the board no matter how well you clean it.

colander   A large perforated bowl-shaped object with handles, used in draining vegetables or lettuce.

egg slicer   A wonderful device for perfectly slicing a hard-boiled egg. It is a great time-saver.

electric blender   An excellent aid in making salad dressings.

food mill   A utensil used to mash, grate, or purée food. It is a large, round container with removable perforated disks of various sizes through which food is forced by a rotating handle.

garlic press   A small utensil used to crush or purée a clove of garlic.

grater   A four-sided metal (stainless steel is best) utensil with sharp-edged holes and slits for grating and slicing in various sizes.

knives   Three are necessary: a paring knife with a sharp pointed tip, a 6-to-8-inch slicing knife, and a 10-to-12-inch chopping knife.

peppermill   Indispensable tool for making and serving salad —the flavor of the fresh ground peppercorns is unequalled. Peppermills are made of all kinds of materials, such as wood, glass, plastic, sterling silver, and porcelain. Peppermills are usually small enough to use at the table and can be adjusted to grind finely or coarsely.

potato peelers   Efficient devices that speed up the task of scraping and peeling vegetables.

salad basket   Wire mesh container used for draining salad greens.

salad bowls   Obviously essential equipment, salad bowls are also a great source of controversy among salad gourmets. The controversy concerns wooden bowls versus all other kinds of bowls. I prefer glass, porcelain, pottery, or even plastic bowls, all of which are abundant. Most of the anti-wooden salad bowl people oppose wooden bowls because they are difficult to clean and care for properly. I oppose them because lettuce and other greens, all of which wilt easily, need to be kept in a cold bowl. For this reason, glass or porcelain is best. Whichever one is your choice, you will find numerous shapes, colors, and sizes from which to choose.

salad fork *and* spoon   Vital when serving and tossing salads, they should be as light as possible so they will be gentle to delicate greens.

shears   An essential tool for snipping chives or parsley.

strainers   Mesh hemispheres used for draining or straining. You will need three sizes.

wire whisks   One small and one medium-sized whisk are perfect for mixing salad dressings.

Appetizers

Certain salads are perfect appetizers, since they are especially light foods. Trying a new salad as an appetizer is also a good opportunity to test it. Fish and egg salads make particularly good starters. The number of dishes needed will depend on the number of guests for dinner: generally allow ½ cup of salad per serving or 3-5 tidbits per person.

Appearance is always important in salads, but this is especially true when placing salad hors d'oeuvres on the coffee table. Garnishes should be very fresh and beautiful to the eye.

HERRING AND CUCUMBER SALAD

2 *jars herring in wine sauce, 8-ounce size*
1 *small red onion, sliced thin*
1 *large cucumber, peeled and sliced thin*
1 *teaspoon sugar*

Combine ingredients; cover, and refrigerate for 2 hours.

Serves 6.

HERRING AND BEET SALAD

Here is an easy and inexpensive salad, which is a great company appetizer.

2 *jars Vita herring, 8-ounce size, drained and chopped*
2 *cups chopped cooked beets (canned are fine)*
1 *cup chopped apple*
1 *small onion, chopped*
¼ *cup red wine vinegar*
1 *tablespoon sugar*
¼ *cup water*
⅓ *cup heavy cream*
  salt and pepper to taste

Combine herring, beets, apple, and onion in a bowl. Blend wine vinegar, sugar, water, and stir into herring mixture. Add heavy cream, and thoroughly mix. Season to taste. Chill until ready to serve.

Serves 6 to 8.

CAPONATA

½ *cup olive oil*
1 *large eggplant, peeled and cubed*
1 *large green pepper, chopped*
1 *zucchini, chopped*
1 *clove garlic, crushed*

2 *medium-sized onions, chopped*
3 *stalks celery, chopped*
3 *tomatoes, peeled and chopped*
¼ *pound mushrooms, chopped*
¼ *cup red wine vinegar*
½ *teaspoon dried oregano*
½ *teaspoon dried basil*
½ *teaspoon sugar*
1 *teaspoon salt*
   freshly grated pepper to taste

Heat olive oil, and sauté eggplant, green pepper, zucchini, garlic, onion, and celery for 10 minutes. Add remaining ingredients, and stir until well combined; cook for about 30 minutes or until most of the liquid is absorbed. Cool mixture, and chill well.

Serves 8 to 10 as appetizer or 6 to 8 as salad.

CAVIAR AND CHOPPED EGG SALAD

6 *hard-boiled eggs, chopped fine*
⅓ *cup sour cream*
1 *tablespoon grated onion*
2 *tablespoons celery, finely chopped*
2 *ounces black caviar*

Combine ingredients, and serve immediately. Accompany with toast triangles.

Serves 6 to 8 as appetizer or 4 as salad.

CURRIED TUNA SALAD

1 *can solid white-meat tuna, 7-ounce size*
1 *package cream cheese, 3-ounce size*
2 *tablespoons sesame seeds*
2 *tablespoons curry powder*
1 *tablespoon soy sauce*
2 *tablespoons milk*

Mix ingredients thoroughly. Serve as dip for toast or crackers, or as filling for celery sticks.

Serves 6 to 8.

TUNA PATE

½ cup chicken broth
2 envelopes unflavored gelatin
2 cans tuna, 7-ounce size, drained
1 cup sour cream
1 tablespoon lemon juice
2 tablespoons grated onion
1 tablespoon finely chopped dill weed
watercress (garnish)

Put the chicken broth in a small sauce pan, and stir in gelatin. Soak for a few minutes. Heat and stir until gelatin dissolves. Set aside. Put remaining ingredients in electric blender, and blend until smooth. Pour into bowl, and stir in dissolved gelatin. Blend well, and pour into loaf pan. Chill until firm. Unmold on serving dish. Garnish with watercress.

Serves 6 to 8 as appetizer or 4 as salad.

JOYCE BUCHMAN'S SALMON MOUSSE

This is a lovely appetizer accompanied with sliced pumpernickel.

1 package unflavored gelatin
2½ tablespoons lemon juice
4 scallions, chopped
½ cup boiling water
¼ teaspoon garlic salt
¼ cup mayonnaise
¼ teaspoon paprika
1 teaspoon dried dill weed

1 *pound salmon,* boned and skinned
(if using canned salmon, drain)*
1 *cup heavy cream, whipped*

Put gelatin, lemon juice, scallions, and boiling water in blender container. Blend at high speed for 30 seconds. Add remaining ingredients, except heavy cream, and blend until smooth, about 30 seconds. Pour mixture into a large bowl, and fold in whipped cream. Pour into lightly oiled quart mold, and set until firm.

Serves 6.
*Tuna may be substituted for salmon.

RATATOUILLE

A traditional dish of southern France, this version of ratatouille is best when chilled. It is also an excellent side dish, served with a simple roast. Either way serve with a crusty French bread.

½ *cup olive oil*
 1 *large onion, thinly sliced*
 2 *cloves garlic, crushed*
 1 *medium-large eggplant, pared and cut into cubes*
 3 *medium-sized zucchini, sliced into ¼-inch pieces, then cut in half*
 3 *large tomatoes, peeled and chopped coarsely*
 1 *large green pepper, chopped*
¼ *cup dry white wine or vermouth*
 1 *tablespoon chopped parsley*
½ *teaspoon dried basil*
 1 *teaspoon salt*
   pepper to taste

Heat ¼ cup olive oil in a large kettle, and sauté onion and garlic for about 5 minutes, until limp and transparent. Push to one side, and add remaining oil and eggplant; cook for 10 minutes, stirring occasionally. Add remaining ingredients, and cook over low heat for about 40 minutes, stirring often. Cool, and refrigerate for at least 3 hours or overnight.

Serves 6.

RAW ASPARAGUS

1½ *pounds raw asparagus*
1 *cup sour cream dressing (see index)*

Wash asparagus and trim ends. Pare off tough skin with vegetable peeler, and arrange in attractive dish. Serve with sour cream dressing on the side.

Serves 6.

PIMIENTO CHEESE CELERY STALKS

24 *celery stalks, trimmed to 4-inch lengths*
1 *package cream cheese, 8-ounce size*
1 *jar pimientos, 4-ounce size, minced*
1 *small onion, minced*
2 *tablespoons pickle relish*
1 *can large black olives, 16-ounce size*

Cream together cream cheese, pimientos, onion, and relish. Fill center of celery sticks, and arrange on serving dish. Garnish with a border of black olives.

Serves 8 to 12.

CALIFORNIA FROZEN TOMATO SALAD

     1 *large can V-8 juice*
  1½ *cups mayonnaise*
  1½ *cups grated onion*
     2 *tablespoons Worcestershire sauce*
        good dash Tabasco sauce
        salt and pepper

Combine ingredients, and blend until smooth. Freeze until slightly frozen but not hard. Scoop onto crisp lettuce cups, and serve with extra mayonnaise.

Serves 8 to 10.

GUACAMOLE SALAD

     2 *ripe avocados, peeled and pitted*
     2 *cloves garlic, crushed*
     2 *tablespoons lemon juice*
     1 *small onion, minced*
   ½ *teaspoon salt*
     1 *small green pepper, chopped fine*
     1 *cucumber, peeled, seeded, and chopped fine*
     1 *large tomato, chopped*
        dash Tabasco sauce
        pepper to taste
        crisp lettuce leaves (garnish)

Mash avocados with back of fork, and add remaining ingredients except for lettuce leaves. Mix well, and check seasoning. Heap in equal portions onto 4 individual serving dishes lined with crisp lettuce leaves.

Serves 4.

HARD-BOILED EGGS
STUFFED WITH MEAT SALAD

6 *hard-boiled eggs, cooled*
2 *tablespoons buttermilk*
1 *tablespoon mayonnaise*
1 *teaspoon prepared mustard*
2 *tablespoons finely chopped celery*
½ *cup finely chopped, cooked tongue*
  salt and pepper to taste
  paprika
  lettuce leaves (for garnish)

Cut hard-boiled eggs in half, and remove yolks. Place yolks in bowl, and combine with buttermilk, mayonnaise, mustard, celery, tongue, and salt and pepper to taste. Fill egg white halves with mixture, sprinkle with paprika, and arrange on serving dish lined with lettuce greens.

Serves 4 to 6.

LES CRUDITES DE SAISON AVEC LES
CHAMPIGNONS A LA GRECQUE

Crudités, or fresh vegetables finely cut, is really a French dish, but I first discovered this delightful plate of crisp fresh vegetables in a charming restaurant in London's Covent Garden.

  bunch of fresh watercress, washed and stemmed
2 *cups cherry tomatoes*
1 *large green pepper, cut into thin, 2-inch long strips*
6 *large carrots, peeled and cut into thin, 2-inch long strips*
6 *stalks celery, cleaned and cut into thin, 2-inch long strips*
½ *pound fresh mushrooms*
1 *cup cooked beets, cut into julienne strips*
½ *cup French Dressing (see index)*

Arrange watercress in center of large round serving platter. Surround with groups of the remaining ingredients. Sprinkle French dressing over all.

Serves 6.

PARTY TUNA BALLS

2 *cans tuna, 7-ounce size, drained and flaked*
3 *stalks celery, finely chopped*
¼ *cup grated cucumber*
½ *teaspoon paprika*
¼ *cup French Dressing (see index)*
2 *tablespoons mayonnaise*
   salt and pepper to taste
1 *cup ground, toasted almonds*
   Bibb lettuce (for garnish)

Combine tuna, celery, cucumber, paprika, French dressing, mayonnaise, and salt and pepper to taste. Form into 2-inch balls and roll in ground almonds. Serve on Bibb lettuce leaves.

Serves 4.

Green Salads

A salad of greens with a simple vinaigrette dressing is an element of classic French cuisine. Served after the entrée and just before the cheese and dessert, it is meant to cleanse the palate. Whether you are planning a family supper or a formal dinner, you can never go wrong serving such a salad. Its variation comes from the great number of greens that may be combined to make this simple yet delicious course. Some are easier and less expensive to find, so experiment with a variety of contrasting colors, flavors, and textures to find the greens that you think make the most interesting and tastiest salads.

Lettuce greens are usually thought of as the main ingredient in a salad, which is not always the case, as this book will prove. Lettuce can be just another ingredient in a tossed or mixed salad, and it also serves as a marvelous garnish for salad molds or fruit salads.

The selection and care of salad greens are essential to good saladmaking. Always buy fresh lettuce, never that which is limp or bruised. Wash separated greens quickly under cold, running water. Do not soak them in water. Drain by lightly shaking and resting greens in colander. (Some people prefer a wire basket for shaking off excess water. To my mind, that process does not work very well, and it may damage the delicate greens.) Next, place cleaned leaves in paper towels or a clean kitchen towel, and pat dry. The leaves can then be rolled in a kitchen towel or placed in a plastic bag and chilled in the crisp section of the refrigerator until ready to use.

To serve, lettuce should be torn into bite-sized or slightly larger pieces. Some lettuce, such as iceberg or Chinese cabbage, can be sliced or shredded. A cup of greens per person is the usual serving.

arugola   Arugola is a slightly peppery lettuce green. Its leaves resemble the dandelion, but are more rounded. Italian in origin, it is not easy to find in markets, but the search is well worth the effort. A delicious salad can be made of arugola and Belgian endive with vinaigrette dressing.

Bibb (limestone)   Bibb is a soft, small head lettuce with delicate deep green leaves. It is the most elegant lettuce and has an excellent though mild flavor.

Boston (butterhead)   Boston lettuce has soft leaves that separate easily and is pale green in color. This slightly sweet lettuce serves as a perfect lining for salad or fruit molds.

curly endive (chicory)   Curly endive has narrow curly leaves, and the color ranges from dark green on the outer leaves to light yellow at the heart. It has a slightly bitter taste. Most frequently, it is used in fruit salads or as a garnish for molds or fruit salads.

Belgian endive (French endive or witloof)   Belgian endive is a white, tightly packed, 4-6-inch head. Extremely elegant and rather bitter, it makes a superior addition to any salad and is delicious served alone with Basic French Dressing.

Chinese cabbage (celery cabbage) Chinese cabbage slightly resembles cabbage and celery in flavor. Its outer leaves are pale green with white inner leaves. It is quite good raw in mixed or tossed salads, and has a lovely velvet texture.

escarole Escarole has a slightly bitter taste, somewhat like Belgian endive. Its curly, broad leaves vary in color from dark green to pale yellow. Escarole has a nice crunch to it, and it is a hearty lettuce.

iceberg (head lettuce) Iceberg is the most popular and plentiful lettuce. It is a solid head lettuce with light green leaves that tightly overlap. This lettuce makes good lettuce cups and serves well as an under-garnish for mixed salads. Its flavor is mild and slightly sweet.

leaf lettuce Leaf lettuce has fragile, light green, curly leaves. It is often grown in home gardens very successfully. The flavor of leaf lettuce is similar to the sweet taste of Bibb lettuce.

romaine (cos) Romaine lettuce is easily recognized by its elongated head. Its beautiful, long, full-shaped leaves have a slightly heavy rib running down the middle. Romaine's flavor is slightly nutty, and it is very crisp and juicy. It is often used in main course salads.

dandelion greens Dandelion leaves, when young, make a delicious salad. They have a tart and bitter flavor.

spinach Dark green, raw spinach makes a fine salad. It must be thoroughly washed, crisped, and stemmed before using.

watercress Watercress has a wonderful peppery flavor. Its dark green, small leaves make a superb garnish and a delicious addition to any salad. Remove stems before using. Watercress is highly perishable, so store it carefully. First, remove the string holding the bunch together and trim off about one inch of the stems. Place loosely in a wide glass or bowl containing about one inch of water.

Other salad greens include celery leaves, beet greens, fiddleheads, kale, sorrel, and Swiss chard.

GREEN SALAD I

8 *escarole leaves*
1 *small head iceberg lettuce*
1 *small head leaf lettuce*
½ *cup Lorenzo Dressing (see index)*

Tear lettuce into bite-sized pieces and combine with dressing. Serve immediately.

Serves 6.

GREEN SALAD II

1 *head Bibb lettuce*
1 *head Boston lettuce*
1 *small head romaine lettuce*
1 *cup watercress*
½ *cup Blue Cheese Dressing*

Wash lettuce and pat dry. Tear into bite-sized pieces; wrap in paper towels and refrigerate. When ready to serve, place in a salad bowl, and pour the dressing over greens. Gently toss and serve immediately.

Serves 8.

ROMAINE SALAD

Using fresh Parmesan cheese makes all the difference in this salad.

2 *heads romaine lettuce*
3 *cloves garlic, crushed*
½ *cup olive oil*
   salt and pepper to taste
1 *tablespoon Worcestershire sauce*
3 *tablespoons grated Parmesan cheese (fresh if possible)*
1 *egg, lightly beaten*
2 *lemons*
1½ *cups croûtons*

Tear romaine lettuce into bite-sized pieces, and place in a large salad bowl. Blend garlic and oil; then strain over lettuce. Season with salt and pepper. Sprinkle Worcestershire sauce and Parmesan cheese over salad; then drizzle lightly beaten raw egg over top. Next, add the juice from two lemons, and finally, add the croûtons. Toss well, and serve immediately.

Serves 6.

VELVET GREEN SALAD

  1 *small head iceberg lettuce*
  1 *head Bibb lettuce*
  1 *avocado, peeled, pitted, and cut into small balls*
 ¼ *cup olive oil*
  1 *tablespoon wine vinegar*
  2 *tablespoons heavy cream*
 ½ *teaspoon dried basil*
   salt and pepper

Carefully wash and dry both heads of lettuce. Tear it into pieces, and place in bowl with avocado balls. Whisk together remaining ingredients; adjust seasoning, and pour over salad. Gently toss.

Serves 4.

GREEN SALAD WITH LIME DRESSING

  1 *small head iceberg lettuce*
  6 *leaves romaine lettuce*
  1 *head Bibb lettuce*
 ½ *cup Lime French Dressing (see index)*

Carefully wash and dry lettuce leaves; tear into pieces. Place in salad bowl, and add Lime Dressing. Toss gently.

Serves 6 to 8.

ARUGOLA AND ENDIVE SALAD

1 *bunch arugola, washed, dried, and stemmed*
2 *Belgian endive, sliced*
½ *cup Vinaigrette Dressing (see index)*

Lightly toss ingredients, and serve immediately.

Serves 4.

CHINESE CABBAGE SALAD

1 *head Chinese cabbage, sliced*
1 *small red onion, thinly sliced*
1 *small green pepper*
½ *cup Basic French Dressing (see index)*
½ *teaspoon sugar*

Place cabbage, onion, and green pepper together in a bowl. Pour on French Dressing. Sprinkle sugar over salad, and lightly toss ingredients. Cover and chill for several hours.

Serves 6.

FENNEL SALAD

4 *fennel stalks*
2 *stalks celery, sliced*
1 *cup shredded lettuce*
⅓ *cup olive oil*
2 *tablespoons lemon juice*
¼ *teaspoon dry mustard*
   pinch sugar
¼ *teaspoon salt*
   pepper to taste

Slice fennel stalks very thin, and place them in a bowl with celery and lettuce. Mix dressing ingredients; pour over salad, and toss.

Serves 4.

Tossed Salads

Tossed salads are probably the most popular salad dish in the United States. Usually heavier than a green salad, tossed salads, in addition to being the perennially popular American dinner salad, can also stand alone as luncheon or dinner main dishes.

There are endless combinations, and a little imagination on the cook's part can produce a variety of exciting new salads. Nearly any food can go into a tossed salad provided it complements the others. Try combining greens with vegetables, cheeses, meats, poultry, and fruit to create your own version of tossed salad. Croutons, nuts, or bacon make exciting finishing touches to these salads.

Unlike a green salad, which should usually be served with Basic French Dressing, tossed salads can be served with any number of varied dressings. Add the dressing just before serving, and toss gently, making sure each ingredient is lightly coated. Tossing the salad and dressing can be done in the kitchen or at the table.

If you are using tomatoes, add them last or use them as garnish because they release a liquid that can weaken salad dressing and make it watery.

TOSSED SALAD

1 *small head iceberg lettuce*
1 *small cucumber, peeled and sliced about ⅛-inch thick*
1 *tomato, cut into wedges*
3 *scallions, sliced*
½ *cup Basic French Dressing (see index)*

Break lettuce leaves into small pieces, and place in salad bowl with cucumber, tomato, and scallions. Pour dressing over salad, and gently toss.

Serves 4.

ITALIAN TOSSED SALAD

1 *head romaine lettuce, broken into bite-sized pieces*
1 *tomato, chopped*
½ *cup stuffed green olives, sliced*
1 *small onion, sliced thin*
2 *stalks celery, sliced*
1 *small green pepper, chopped*
½ *cup Italian Dressing (see index)*

Place first 6 ingredients in salad bowl. Pour dressing over salad, and toss.

Serves 4.

BELGIAN ENDIVE AND BACON SALAD

6 *Belgian endive*
4 *scallions, minced*
8 *strips bacon, cooked until crisp and crumbled*
1 *teaspoon bacon drippings*
4 *tablespoons olive oil*
4 *tablespoons tarragon vinegar*
1 *cup garlic croutons*
salt and pepper to taste

Cut endive into ½-inch chunks, and separate leaves in a salad bowl. Add scallions and bacon. Toss lightly. Mix bacon drippings, olive oil, and vinegar; then pour over salad and toss. Add 1 cup garlic croutons; gently toss, and season to taste with salt and pepper.

Serves 4.

PLAIN SPINACH SALAD WITH TART MUSTARD DRESSING

1 *pound leaf spinach*
½ *cup olive oil*
2 *tablespoons red wine vinegar*
1½ *teaspoons prepared mustard*
1 *clove garlic, crushed*
salt and pepper to taste

Wash spinach leaves, and pat dry. Remove stems, and tear leaves into small pieces. Chill thoroughly. Place the spinach in a bowl. Mix remaining ingredients, and pour over the salad and toss.

Serves 6.

SPINACH, MUSHROOM, AND BACON SALAD

1 *pound leaf spinach*
½ *pound mushrooms, thinly sliced*
½ *pound bacon, cooked until crisp and crumbled*
⅔ *cup Garlic Dressing (see index)*

Wash and dry spinach leaves. Remove stems, and tear into small pieces. Place in salad bowl, and top with mushrooms and bacon. Pour Garlic Dressing over salad, and toss.

Serves 6.

MANDARIN ORANGE SALAD
WITH CREAM DRESSING

Salad:
1 *small head romaine lettuce*
1 *cup bite-sized pieces watercress*
1 *can mandarin oranges, 11-ounce size, drained*
    (save 2 tablespoons of liquid for salad dressing)
1 *medium-sized red onion, sliced into thin rings*

Cream dressing:
⅓ *cup vegetable oil*
 1 *tablespoon lemon juice*
 2 *tablespoons mandarin orange liquid*
 2 *tablespoons heavy cream*
    salt and pepper to taste

Tear romaine lettuce and watercress into small pieces, and put into salad bowl with mandarin oranges and sliced onion. Mix dressing, and pour over salad. Gently toss.

Serves 4.

DANDELION AND EGG SALAD

4 *cups dandelion leaves, broken into pieces*
2 *hard-boiled eggs, chopped*
½ *cup Mustard Dressing (see index)*

Toss ingredients well.

Serves 4 to 6.

HAM SALAD

½ *pound sliced, boiled ham, coarsely chopped*
1 *hard-boiled egg, chopped*
1 *small cucumber, peeled, seeded, and chopped*
1 *small green pepper, minced*
1 *tablespoon fresh, chopped parsley*
1 *teaspoon prepared mustard*
1 *tablespoon lemon juice*

⅓ cup vegetable oil
salt and pepper to taste

Combine ham, chopped egg, cucumber, green pepper, and parsley in a large bowl. Blend mustard, lemon juice, and vegetable oil in a small bowl. Pour over salad, and toss. Season with salt and pepper.

Serves 4.

CANTALOUPE TOSSED SALAD

1 cantaloupe, peeled and seeded
2 tomatoes, peeled and seeded
1 cucumber, peeled
⅓ cup vegetable oil
2 tablespoons lemon juice
1 tablespoon fresh, chopped parsley
1 teaspoon chopped mint
1 teaspoon dry mustard
salt and pepper to taste

Cut cantaloupe into bite-sized cubes, and place in large bowl. Cut tomatoes into wedges, and add to bowl with cantaloupe. Cut cucumber in half lengthwise, and cut into ¼-inch thick slices; add to other vegetables, and gently toss. In a small bowl, combine oil, lemon juice, parsley, mint, dry mustard, salt, and pepper to taste. Pour over vegetables, and lightly toss.

Serves 4 to 6.

SALADE JACQUES MICHEL

1 head romaine lettuce, torn into small pieces
2 bananas, peeled and sliced
⅔ cup walnuts
⅓ cup mayonnaise
1 teaspoon lemon juice
¼ teaspoon paprika
½ teaspoon prepared mustard

Place lettuce, bananas, and walnuts in a salad bowl. Blend remaining ingredients in a small bowl. Pour over salad, and toss gently.

Serves 4.

EAST COAST TOSSED SALAD

    1 *bunch watercress*
    1 *head Boston lettuce, cleaned and torn into pieces*
    4 *slices crisp cooked bacon, crumbled*
    6 *radishes, sliced*
    1 *teaspoon fresh snipped chives*
    1 *tablespoon minced sweet onion*
  ½ *cup Vinaigrette Dressing (see index)*

Wash and trim stems from watercress, and place in a bowl. Add bacon, lettuce, radishes, chives, and onion. Pour on dressing. Toss ingredients gently, but thoroughly.

Serves 6.

MARIAN'S PEPPERED SPINACH SALAD

    1 *pound raw spinach, washed, stemmed, and torn into*
      bite-sized pieces
    1 *can mandarin oranges, 10-ounce size, drained*
  ¼ *pound sliced fresh mushrooms*
  ⅓ *cup olive oil*
    2 *tablespoons red wine vinegar*
  ½ *teaspoon dry mustard*
  ½ *teaspoon salt*
    1 *teaspoon freshly ground pepper*

Place spinach, mandarin oranges, and mushrooms in salad bowl. Whisk together remaining ingredients, and pour over salad. Toss and serve.

Serves 6.

SEAFOOD CHEF'S SALAD

1 *quart lettuce leaves, broken into pieces*
1 *pound shrimp, cooked and cooled*
½ *pound crabmeat, cooked and cooled*
1 *pound poached bass, cooked and cut into bite-sized pieces*
3 *hard-boiled eggs, quartered*
16 *cherry tomatoes*
¾ *cup Caper Mayonnaise (see index)*

Line a salad bowl with the lettuce; arrange shrimp, crabmeat, bass, hard-boiled eggs, and cherry tomatoes attractively on top. Pour Caper Dressing over salad, and toss.

Serves 8.

JULIENNE CHEESE SALAD

4 *ounces cheddar cheese, sliced and cut into julienne strips*
4 *ounces sliced Swiss cheese, cut into julienne strips*
4 *ounces Muenster cheese, sliced and cut into julienne strips*
½ *cup chopped green stuffed olives*
½ *teaspoon celery seeds*
⅓ *cup mayonnaise*
1 *tablespoon lemon juice*
½ *teaspoon fresh ground pepper*
salt to taste
lettuce (for garnish)

Combine ingredients through olives in a large bowl. Mix remaining ingredients in small bowl. Then toss lightly with cheese mixture. Chill thoroughly. Serve on lettuce greens.

Serves 4.

Tomato Salads

The tomato, whose fame has ranged from that of "love apple" to that of a poisonous fruit, has certainly won the right to a category of its own among salads.

It plays a colorful supporting role in tossed salads, serves as a container for seafood and other filler salads—and is incomparable by itself with a small amount of Basic French Dressing drizzled over it. Tomatoes have an affinity with basil, and you may want to add it to any dressing used with tomatoes, when possible.

The most important thing to remember when preparing a tomato salad is to use ripe tomatoes with good color. Unfortunately, one cannot always get nice garden tomatoes, and I almost prefer using canned tomatoes, but they must be drained very carefully and aren't as attractive, though the flavor is far better than the firm orangish supermarket variety. By all means, grow tomatoes yourself if you are lucky enough to have the space in your backyard. They grow easily if they have plenty of sun and water.

In London's Cordon Bleu and Paris's, too, we always peel the tomato before using it, but you don't have to do that, especially in tossed salads. I like them peeled because it is easier to enjoy their velvet texture. To peel tomatoes simply immerse them one at a time in boiling water for 7 or 8 seconds and remove immediately. With the sharp tip of a pointed small knife the peel will come right off.

DANISH-STYLE TOMATOES

This salad is particularly attractive served in a glass bowl.

½ cup vegetable oil
2 tablespoons wine vinegar
3 tablespoons crumbled Danish blue cheese
1 clove garlic, crushed
½ teaspoon salt
  pepper to taste
  pinch of sugar
6 ripe tomatoes
  parsley (for garnish)

Make a dressing by beating all ingredients except tomatoes together in a bowl or using a blender. Slice tomatoes, and arrange them in a shallow serving dish. Pour the blue cheese dressing over the tomatoes; cover, and let stand for 30 minutes. Sprinkle with chopped fresh parsley before serving.

Serves 8 to 10.

SERBIAN SALAD

This salad is probably more French than Yugoslavian, but when I spent several weeks in a southern seaside resort of Yugoslavia, they served us this salad nearly every day and called it Serbian Salad. It is a favorite of mine.

4 medium-large tomatoes
1 medium-sized onion, minced
¼ cup finely chopped parsley
½ cup vegetable oil
3 tablespoons wine vinegar
⅛ teaspoon dry mustard
  salt and pepper to taste

First, place four individual salad plates in front of you. Thinly slice each tomato and arrange one sliced tomato across each plate. In bowl put remaining ingredients and beat with wire whisk. Adjust seasoning and spoon in equal amounts over sliced tomatoes.

Serves 4.

Note: For variety, place the sliced tomatoes on crisp lettuce leaves or watercress, and add ½ teaspoon basil to dressing. Fresh grated Parmesan cheese sprinkled on top of tomatoes after salad dressing is also delicious.

ZUCCHINI, TOMATO, AND BASIL SALAD

Salad:
4 *medium-sized zucchini, sliced about ¼-inch thick*
3 *firm, ripe, medium-sized tomatoes, sliced about ¼-inch thick*
1 *large red onion, chopped*

Dressing:
½ *cup olive oil*
 3 *tablespoons wine vinegar*
 2 *cloves garlic, crushed*
 1 *tablespoon fresh chopped basil*
   or
 1 *teaspoon dried basil*
¼ *teaspoon dry mustard*
½ *teaspoon salt*
   pepper to taste

Place zucchini, tomatoes, and chopped onion in a large bowl. In a separate bowl, blend dressing with wire whisk. Pour over salad, and cover. Refrigerate for several hours; overnight is best.

Serves 6.

COOKED GREEN BEAN AND TOMATO SALAD

 1 *pound green beans, trimmed and cut into 1-inch lengths*
¼ *cup olive oil*

1 *medium-sized onion, chopped*
1 *cup chopped tomatoes*
½ *teaspoon dried oregano*
1 *tablespoon lemon juice*
½ *teaspoon salt*
 pepper to taste

Heat olive oil. Sauté onion for 5 minutes. Add green beans; cover, and simmer for 5 minutes. Add remaining ingredients, and cook for 15 minutes more. Cool and refrigerate for several hours or overnight.

Serves 4 to 6.

HARLEQUIN SALAD

1 *pint cherry tomatoes, cut in half*
1 *can large black olives, 16-ounce size, pitted and halved*
2 *cups raw cauliflower, broken into small flowerets and pieces*
½ *cup Garlic Dressing (see index)*

Combine tomatoes, olives, and cauliflower. Gently mix in salad dressing. Chill thoroughly before serving.

Serves 6.

TOMATO AND SWISS CHEESE SALAD
WITH YOGURT DRESSING

¼ *pound Swiss cheese slices, cut julienne style*
1 *small green pepper, chopped*
3 *hard-boiled eggs, chopped*
½ *cup plain yogurt*
1 *small clove garlic, crushed (optional)*
½ *teaspoon lemon juice*
 salt and pepper to taste
2 *tomatoes, sliced*

In a bowl, combine Swiss cheese, green pepper, eggs, yogurt, garlic, lemon juice, salt and pepper. Arrange equal portions of tomato slices on four salad plates, and pile mixed ingredients over tomatoes.

Serves 4.

TOMATO CUPS

2 *cups canned chickpeas, drained*
3 *tablespoons fresh, chopped parsley*
1 *clove garlic, crushed*
1 *tablespoon chopped capers*
1 *tablespoon lemon juice*
3 *tablespoons olive oil*
  salt and pepper to taste
4 *large, ripe tomatoes*

Combine ingredients, except for tomatoes. Cut tomatoes in half and scoop out tomato pulp. Stir pulp into chickpea mixture, and pile into tomato cups.

Serves 4.

TOMATOES
STUFFED WITH RICE AND SHRIMP

⅓ *cup vegetable oil*
1 *tablespoon red wine vinegar*
1 *raw egg yolk*
½ *teaspoon prepared mustard*
¼ *teaspoon dried basil*
1 *clove garlic, crushed*
  salt and pepper to taste
2 *cups cooked rice*
1 *can, 2¾ ounce size, tiny Danish shrimp*
4 *large tomatoes*

Beat together oil, vinegar, egg yolk, mustard, basil, garlic, and salt and pepper. Pour over rice and shrimp. Gently combine. Cut tops off tomatoes, and scoop out tomato pulp. Add pulp to rice mixture, and blend. Fill each tomato with mixture.

Serves 4.

TOMATO FANS

1 *cup cottage cheese*
3 *tablespoons sour cream*
2 *scallions, finely chopped*
½ *cup grated cucumber*
1 *stalk celery, finely chopped*
1 *tablespoon soy sauce*
1 *small clove garlic, crushed*
  salt and pepper to taste
4 *large tomatoes*
  crisp lettuce leaves

Combine all ingredients except tomatoes and lettuce. Place tomatoes on stem ends. Cut down but not through tomatoes in places on their tops about ¾ inch apart. Push tomatoes open. Fill with a tablespoon or two of the mixture. Place on crisp lettuce leaves.

Serves 4.

Entrées

A salad is always a surprising and welcome lunch or dinner, and it can easily provide a well-balanced meal. Soup, cold cuts, and a variety of bread and rolls are good accompaniments, along with dessert. These meals are often economical—and good for dieters, too. A main course salad can be a sumptuous lobster salad, a hearty bean salad, a meat-and-potatoes salad, or a molded salad, to name a few possibilities. The menus at the back of the book will help you plan meals around salads.

The flavor of main-dish salads can often be improved by marinating; refrigerate for at least one hour, until just before serving, unless directed otherwise in a recipe.

Leftovers, such as turkey, roast beef or chicken, are easy to utilize in main-dish salads.

Whatever you choose, just be sure to think of salads when putting together a menu that has a unique twist.

SHRIMP GAZPACHO

3 *ripe tomatoes, chopped*
1 *medium-sized onion, chopped*
1 *cucumber, chopped*
2 *cloves garlic, chopped*
½ *cup tomato juice*
2 *tablespoons olive oil*
3 *tablespoons vinegar*
  dash Tabasco sauce
  salt and pepper
1 *green pepper, chopped*
12 *black olives, cut into slivers*
1 *pound cooked shrimp, chopped coarsely*
2 *tablespoons fresh, chopped parsley*

Place tomatoes, onion, cucumber, garlic, tomato juice, olive oil, vinegar, and Tabasco sauce in a blender and purée for 30 seconds. Season with salt and pepper. Place in a large bowl with green pepper, olives, and shrimp. Chill thoroughly. Adjust seasoning, and garnish with chopped parsley.

Serves 4.

RICH SHRIMP AND DILL SALAD

Shrimp salad always seems to be overloaded with celery. Not this one—here is a pure shrimp salad. It is delicious accompanied by avocado slices or artichoke hearts and black bread.

2 *pounds boiled, medium-sized shrimp*
¾ *cup mayonnaise*
1 *tablespoon lemon juice*
1 *tablespoon finely minced dill*
1 *teaspoon fresh, chopped parsley*
2 *tablespoons grated onion*
  salt and pepper to taste

Combine ingredients, and chill for at least 1 hour.

Serves 4.

VENICE CHICKEN SALAD

2 *packages frozen peas and carrots, 10-ounce size*
1 *cup cubed, boiled potatoes*
1 *cup chopped, cooked chicken*
½ *cup mayonnaise*
1 *tablespoon lemon juice*
1 *teaspoon chopped parsley*
   salt and pepper
6 *small sweet pickles*
   lettuce leaves (for garnish)

Cook packages of frozen peas and carrots; drain and cool. Place them in a bowl with potatoes, chicken, mayonnaise, lemon juice, and parsley. Season with salt and pepper. Chill thoroughly. Pile salad on a serving dish lined with crisp lettuce leaves. Slice pickles lengthwise, and make a border by standing them up against the salad.

Serves 4.

SPICY CURRIED CHICKEN SALAD

2 *large chicken breasts, halved*
2 *stalks celery, sliced, plus ½ cup minced celery*
2 *carrots, sliced*
1 *medium-sized onion, chopped*
4 *peppercorns*
1 *bay leaf*
½ *teaspoon salt*
1 *small green pepper, chopped fine*
1 *cup diced apple*
¼ *cup minced scallions*
¾ *cup mayonnaise*
1 *teaspoon lemon juice*
   dash Tabasco sauce
1 *tablespoon curry powder*
   salt and pepper

In a large saucepan, place chicken breasts, celery, carrots, onion, peppercorns, bay leaf, and salt. Cover with water; bring to a boil; reduce heat to a simmer, and cook for 20 minutes. Cool, then skin and bone. Cut the chicken into bite-sized pieces. Transfer the chicken to a large bowl with green pepper, ½ cup minced celery, apple, and scallions. In a small bowl, combine mayonnaise, lemon juice, Tabasco sauce, and curry powder. Pour this mixture over the chicken, and combine. Check seasoning. Chill for several hours.

Serves 4 to 6.

CREAMY CHICKEN TARRAGON SALAD

2 *large chicken breasts*
3½ *cups water*
½ *cup dry, white wine*
1 *bay leaf*
1 *stalk celery, chopped*
1 *carrot, chopped*
1 *onion, sliced*
4 *peppercorns*
½ *teaspoon salt*
½ *cup mayonnaise*
2 *tablespoons heavy cream*
1 *teaspoon lemon juice*
1 *teaspoon dry tarragon*

Combine water and wine. Add bay leaf, celery, carrot, onion, peppercorns, and salt. Bring to a boil. Add chicken breasts; cover, and simmer for 20 minutes. Remove the chicken from the liquid, and drain while cooling. Remove skin and bones, then cut chicken into bite-sized pieces. Place in bowl. Next, blend mayonnaise with heavy cream, lemon juice, and tarragon. Pour over chicken, and blend thoroughly. Check seasoning; cover, and chill for at least 2 hours.

Serves 4 to 6.

VEAL SALAD

3 *cups diced, cooked veal*
8 *strips crisp, cooked bacon, crumbled*
½ *cup finely chopped celery*
3 *scallions, sliced*
½ *cup mayonnaise*
1 *tablespoon lemon juice*
  crisp lettuce leaves
6 *tomatoes*
1 *tablespoon fresh, chopped parsley*

Combine veal, bacon, celery, scallions, mayonnaise, and lemon juice. Line six salad plates with crisp lettuce leaves, and place a tomato on top. Cut down through each tomato to form quarters, and heap salad on top. Garnish with fresh chopped parsley.

Serves 6.

FANELLI SALAD

2 *cups buttermilk*
1 *cup canned beets, cut into julienne strips*
½ *cup sliced scallions*
1 *clove garlic, crushed*
½ *cup black olive slivers*
1 *small cucumber, cut in half lengthwise, seeds removed, then cubed*
½ *cup chopped celery*
2 *teaspoons dried tarragon*
½ *pound boiled ham, cut into julienne strips*
4 *slices Swiss cheese, cut into julienne strips*
½ *teaspoon salt*
  pepper to taste
1 *large bunch watercress*

Combine ingredients, except for watercress, and chill for 1 hour. Arrange pieces of watercress on the bottom of a large serving dish, and spoon salad into center of dish.

Serves 4.

CAESAR SALAD

Caesar Salad is a well-known salad that originated in California. The combined ingredients do, indeed, produce an excellent flavor. Line up the ingredients on the dinner table and prepare it before your guests with gusto. It is one of my personal favorites.

>   1 *large head romaine lettuce*
>   3 *tablespoons olive oil*
>   1 *clove garlic, crushed*
>   4 *anchovy fillets, chopped*
>   ⅛ *teaspoon salt*
>   *fresh grated pepper to taste*
>   1 *egg, boiled for 1 minute*
>   2 *tablespoons lemon juice*
>   1 *tablespoon Worcestershire sauce*
>   ¼ *cup fresh, grated Parmesan cheese*
>   1 *cup toasted crôutons*

Tear lettuce into bite-sized pieces, and place it in a large salad bowl. In a small bowl, combine olive oil, garlic, anchovy fillets, salt and pepper. Crush with the back of a spoon until well blended. Pour over lettuce and lightly toss. Break egg over salad and toss again. Next, add lemon juice, and Worcestershire sauce. Gently toss. Finally, sprinkle Parmesan cheese and croutons over salad and toss. Serve immediately.

Serves 4.

CHEF'S SALAD

>   1 *quart mixed lettuce pieces*
>   1 *cup watercress pieces*
>   1½ *cups cooked, cubed beef*
>   4 *slices Swiss cheese, cut into julienne strips*
>   4 *ounces cheddar cheese, cut into cubes*
>   ½ *pound boiled ham, cut into julienne strips*
>   1 *red onion, sliced thin*
>   2 *tomatoes, cut into wedges*
>   2 *hard-boiled eggs, quartered*

½ *cup Vinaigrette Dressing (see index)*

Combine lettuce and watercress in such a way as to cover the bottom of a large salad bowl. Arrange remaining solid ingredients attractively on top. Just before serving, pour Vinaigrette Dressing over salad.

Serves 4.

MIXED MEAT SALAD

To round out the meal, serve with sliced tomatoes and assorted rolls or bread with butter.

- ½ *pound roast beef, sliced and cut into julienne strips*
- ½ *pound boiled ham, sliced and cut into julienne strips*
- ½ *pound sliced tongue, cut into julienne strips*
- ½ *cup finely chopped dill pickles*
- 2 *cups diced cooked potatoes*
- ⅓ *cup oil*
- 2 *tablespoons vinegar*
- 1 *tablespoon dill pickle liquid from pickle jar*
- 1 *teaspoon prepared mustard*
- 1 *clove garlic, crushed*
  salt and pepper to taste

Place roast beef, ham, tongue, pickles, and potatoes in a large bowl. In a separate bowl, blend the remaining ingredients well, and pour over salad. Toss, and chill for an hour.

Serves 6.

POACHED EGGS IN ASPIC

- 4 *poached eggs*
- 3 *scallions, sliced*
- 1 *green pepper, minced*
- 1 *tomato, peeled, juice squeezed out, then diced*
- 2 *boiled potatoes, diced*
- 1 *quart canned jellied consommé*
  fresh chopped parsley for garnish
  dash freshly ground pepper

Place poached eggs on the bottom of four soup cups. Divide the scallions, pepper, tomato, and potatoes evenly, and spoon equal portions over each egg. Pour 1 cup consommé in each cup, and refrigerate until firm. Either eat from cup, or unmold and sprinkle with fresh chopped parsley and freshly ground pepper.

Serves 4.

HOT TUNA SUPPER SALAD

4 *medium-sized potatoes*
2 *tablespoons butter*
2 *stalks celery, finely chopped*
1 *small green pepper, finely chopped*
1 *medium-sized onion, chopped*
2 *cans tuna, 7-ounce size, drained*
½ *cup Basic French Dressing (see index)*
salt and pepper to taste

Boil potatoes in their jackets until tender; drain. When the potatoes are cool enough to handle, peel and slice them. Heat the butter in a skillet, and sauté the celery, green pepper, and onion for 5 minutes. Add slightly flaked tuna, potatoes, and Basic French Dressing. Gently combine; simmer until heated through. Season with salt and pepper.

Serves 6.

COLD TONGUE SALAD

2 *cups cooked diced tongue*
1 *cup cold, cooked green beans, cut into 1-inch lengths*
½ *cup Basic French Dressing with fines herbes (see index)*
1 *tomato, chopped*
½ *cup chopped, stuffed green olives*
1 *small, red onion, sliced thin*
1 *head iceberg lettuce*
Cheddar cheese sticks

Marinate tongue and green beans in dressing for 1 hour, covered in refrigerator. Add tomato, green olives, and onion. Toss. Line salad bowl with lettuce, and heap salad on top. Garnish with cheddar cheese sticks.

Serves 4.

LOBSTER TARRAGON SALAD

1 *pound lobster meat, cut into bite-sized pieces*
½ *cup mayonnaise*
2 *tablespoons lemon juice*
1 *teaspoon tarragon*
1 *teaspoon minced onion*
   salt and pepper to taste

Blend ingredients well, and serve on crisp lettuce leaves.

Serves 4.

CITY LOBSTER SALAD

1 *head romaine lettuce, torn into pieces*
2 *cups escarole, torn into pieces*
3 *cups lobster meat, cut into bite-sized pieces*
4 *scallions, sliced*
1 *cup chopped celery*
1 *avocado, peeled and cubed*
2 *tomatoes, cubed*
6 *large, stuffed green olives, sliced*
⅔ *cup Vinaigrette Dressing (see index)*

Place all ingredients except Vinaigrette Dressing in a large bowl. Mix together gently. Pour vinaigrette sauce over mixture, and lightly toss again.

Serves 4.

HOT AND COLD CHILI SALAD

2 *tablespoons butter*
1 *medium-sized onion, chopped*
1 *clove garlic, crushed*
1 *pound ground round steak*
1 *can whole tomatoes, 16-ounce size, undrained*
1 *can chili con carne with beans, 16-ounce size*
2 *tablespoons chili powder*
1 *teaspoon cumin*
   dash Tabasco sauce
½ *teaspoon salt*
   pepper to taste
1 *large head shredded lettuce*
1 *package corn chips, 6-ounce size*
4 *ounces grated cheddar cheese*
½ *cup sliced scallions*

Melt butter; sauté onion and garlic in it for 5 minutes. Add meat, and break up with fork. Cook until meat is browned. Add tomatoes, chili con carne, chili powder, cumin, Tabasco sauce, salt and pepper. Stir and cook for about 30 minutes. Adjust seasoning. Serve on individual salad plates: on each plate, arrange a cup of shredded lettuce and a handful of corn chips. Spoon equal portions of chili over each salad. Generously sprinkle with grated cheddar cheese and sliced scallions.

Serves 6.

HEALTH FOOD SALAD

3 *cups peeled, grated carrots*
1 *cup chopped, raw spinach*
¾ *cup chopped cabbage*
1 *cup cooked soy beans*
½ *cup raisins*
1 *teaspoon honey*
¼ *cup safflower oil*
1 *tablespoon lemon juice*
1 *tablespoon water*

½ *teaspoon seasoned salt*
salt and pepper to taste

Place carrots, spinach, cabbage, soy beans, and raisins in a large bowl. In a separate bowl, mix the honey, oil, lemon juice, water, seasoned salt, and salt and pepper to taste. Add to other salad ingredients, and toss.

Serves 4 to 6.

HOT DOG SALAD

1 *package elbow macaroni, 8-ounce size*
6 *hot dogs, boiled and cooled*
1 *cup shredded cheddar cheese*
1 *small green pepper, chopped fine*
2 *pimientos, chopped*
1 *can peas, 8-ounce size, drained*
3 *scallions, sliced*
½ *teaspoon salt*
pepper to taste
½ *cup mayonnaise*
1 *tablespoon vinegar*
dash Tabasco sauce

Cook macaroni according to package directions; drain, and cool slightly. Slice hot dogs into ¼-inch rounds, and place in a bowl with macaroni. Add the remaining ingredients, and blend well.

Serves 6 to 8.

SALMON SALAD

1 *pound canned salmon, drained, boned and skinned*
1 *tablespoon chopped capers*
½ *cup diced celery*
2 *tablespoons chopped green pepper*
1 *tablespoon lemon juice*
½ *cup mayonnaise*
½ *teaspoon salt*
pepper to taste

Combine ingredients, and chill. Serve on crisp lettuce leaves or as sandwich filling.

Serves 4.

CRABMEAT SUPREME

1 *pound crabmeat*
1 *can artichoke hearts, 14-ounce size, drained and quartered*
½ *green pepper, chopped*
½ *cup chopped celery*
2 *hard-boiled eggs, chopped*
1 *cup cherry tomatoes, halved*
2 *cups cooked rice, cooled*
¾ *cup Thousand Island Dressing (see index)*
lettuce (for garnish)

Combine ingredients. Line a salad bowl with lettuce greens and heap salad on top.

Serves 6.

SWISS CHEESE SALAD

¾ *pound Swiss cheese, cut into julienne strips*
3 *hard-boiled eggs*
¼ *cup chopped, stuffed green olives*
½ *cup mayonnaise*
¼ *cup sour cream*
1 *teaspoon prepared mustard*
1 *small onion, grated*
salt and pepper to taste
lettuce leaves (for garnish)

Combine ingredients, and chill for at least 1 hour. Serve on crisp lettuce leaves.

Serves 4 to 6.

CURRIED EGG SALAD

8 *hard-boiled eggs, chopped*
1 *cup finely chopped celery*
1 *medium-sized onion, chopped*
¼ *cup plus 2 tablespoons minced green pepper*
½ *cup mayonnaise*
1 *tablespoon lemon juice*
1 *teaspoon curry powder or to taste*
½ *teaspoon salt*
  pepper to taste
  paprika

Gently combine chopped eggs, celery, onion, and ¼ cup green pepper. In a small bowl, blend mayonnaise, lemon juice, and curry powder; season with salt and pepper. Pour over egg mixture, and lightly combine. Heap onto crisp lettuce leaves, and sprinkle with paprika. Decorate the top with remaining green pepper.

Serves 4.

EGG SALAD ITALIAN STYLE

6 *hard-boiled eggs, chopped*
½ *pound bacon, cooked until crisp and crumbled*
8 *ounces mozzarella cheese, diced*
1 *cup chopped celery*
⅔ *cup mayonnaise*
1 *tablespoon lemon juice*
1 *teaspoon Dijon mustard*
½ *teaspoon oregano*
  salt and pepper to taste

Place eggs, bacon, and cheese in a large bowl. Add remaining ingredients, mix well. Serve with toasted garlic bread.

Serves 4.

ZELDA'S HEARTY FISH AND BEAN SALAD

Crusty French bread and sliced tomatoes make this a fine dinner.

1 *pound dried navy beans, cooked*
1 *can tuna, 7-ounce size, drained*
1 *can salmon, 7-ounce size, drained*
1 *green pepper, chopped*
3 *stalks celery, chopped*
6 *giant stuffed olives, chopped*
1 *tablespoon Dijon mustard*
¼ *cup olive oil*
3 *tablespoons dry white wine*
1 *tablespoon lemon juice*
½ *teaspoon oregano*
½ *teaspoon basil*
1 *clove garlic, crushed*
   salt and pepper

Combine ingredients well, and chill for a few hours.

Serves 6.

AVOCADO STUFFED WITH BLUE CHEESE SALAD

4 *ounces crumbled blue cheese*
½ *cup mayonnaise*
2 *pimientos, chopped fine*
2 *avocados, halved and pitted*

Combine blue cheese, mayonnaise, and pimientos. Spoon equal portions of this mixture into avocado halves.

Serves 4.

COLD PECAN CHICKEN SALAD BOWL

Chef José Diaz of the cheerful Ballroom Restaurant in New York's Soho district created this attractive and palatable salad.

    2 large chicken breasts, boned and skinned
      juice of 1 lemon
    ¼ teaspoon salt
    3 tablespoons butter
    ⅓ cup olive oil
    1 tablespoon white wine vinegar
    1 head romaine lettuce pieces, torn into pieces
    1 medium-sized, raw zucchini, grated
    1 carrot, grated
    8 canned artichoke hearts
    8 slices unpeeled cucumber
   12 marinated mushroom caps
   12 black olives
    1 cup pecans
    8 strips pimiento (for garnish)

Halve each boned and skinned chicken breast and cut each half into four long strips. Place in buttered shallow baking dish, sprinkle with lemon juice and salt; dot with 3 tablespoons of butter and cover with lightly oiled waxed paper. Bake in 375°F. oven for 15 minutes, or until tender. Transfer chicken slices to a plate, and pour the juices from the chicken into a blender along with the olive oil and vinegar. Blend for 10 seconds at high speed; pour over chicken, and turn pieces until well coated with sauce. Set aside. Arrange each of four individual salad bowls in the following manner: line bowl with 1 cup romaine lettuce pieces. Sprinkle ¼ of the grated zucchini and carrot over the lettuce. Arrange 2 artichoke hearts, 2 slices cucumber, 3 mushroom caps, and 3 black olives around the border of bowl. Next, place four strips of chicken over the salad, and sprinkle with ¼ cup pecans. Garnish the top with 2 strips pimiento.

Serves 4.

FRESH FISH SALAD

1 *pound lean whitefish, sole, flounder, or cod, poached,
   skinned, boned, and flaked*
2 *tablespoons finely chopped green pepper*
2 *scallions, minced*
1 *tablespoon chopped capers*
½ *cup mayonnaise*
¼ *teaspoon prepared mustard*
1 *tablespoon lemon juice*
   dash Tabasco sauce
   salt and pepper to taste

Put flaked fish, green pepper, scallions, and capers in a bowl, and toss. Blend mayonnaise, mustard, lemon juice, and Tabasco sauce; pour over fish salad. Blend well, and chill.

Serves 4 to 6.

CURRIED MUSSEL SALAD

Serve this with toasted French bread and dry white wine.

3 *pounds mussels, scrubbed and bearded*
½ *cup chopped onion*
½ *cup dry white wine*
1½ *cups water*
1 *tablespoon chopped, fresh parsley*
1 *cup mayonnaise*
2 *scallions, finely chopped*
1 *tablespoon chopped, fresh parsley*
2 *teaspoons curry powder*
1 *clove garlic, crushed*
   dash ginger
1 *tablespoon lemon juice*
   salt and pepper to taste

Place onion, wine, water, and parsley in a large kettle, and bring to a boil. Add mussels; cover, and cook for 8 minutes, or until shells open. Discard any shells that do not open. Remove mussels from shells; drain, and cool. Blend remaining ingredients, and combine with mussels. Cover, then refrigerate for at least 3 hours.

Serves 6.

ROAST BEEF AND POTATO SALAD

This main dish is delicious accompanied by sliced ripe tomatoes, French bread, and red wine.

     6 *potatoes, cooked, peeled, and cubed*
     2 *cups cubed roast beef*
    ½ *cup Vinaigrette Dressing (see index)*
     1 *tablespoon finely chopped fresh parsley*

Combine potatoes and roast beef. Pour over Vinaigrette. Garnish with parsley. Refrigerate for several hours.

Serves 6.

Vegetable and Legume Salads

I could write for days on the virtues of vegetable and bean salads. They are chock full of minerals and vitamins, as well as being money-saving, hearty, and palatable. People in every part of the country can enjoy fresh and frozen vegetables. When they are in season, supermarkets feature fresh vegetables, and accordingly, when vegetables are plentiful, they are also economical—a good buying clue to keep in mind when planning menus.

The salads in this chapter fall into two categories: those made with green or yellow vegetables other than greens, and those made with legumes, which are peas, beans, and lentils.

For best results, always try to use fresh vegetables, unless a recipe specifies that frozen are required. A salad cook's best friend is usually the person who runs the produce department of a grocery store. Cultivate this person by asking him or her to show you how to select vegetables when they are at their peaks. If you are consistent in your efforts (and flattery), you will probably be rewarded with top-quality produce that has been put away especially for you.

There are almost as many methods of cooking fresh vegetables as there are cooks. One method that works particularly well for vegetables that are going into salads is blanching. To blanch, put a large pot of salted water on the stove, and bring to a boil. Toss in the vegetables, and simmer until crisp or done to your taste. Recommended blanching times for vegetables found in recipes in this chapter are listed below:

Artichokes	15 minutes for small; 25 for large
Broccoli	8 minutes for flowerets; 12 minutes for stems
Cauliflower	8 minutes for flowerets; 15 minutes for whole head
Celeriac	8-10 minutes for quartered pieces
Corn	Put into boiling water; cover; remove from heat and let stand 5 minutes
Green beans	6-8 minutes for crisp ones

If you are using frozen vegetables, cook according to package direction, but shorten the cooking time by about 1 minute so the vegetables remain quite crisp.

Most legumes can be purchased canned and pre-cooked; you need only to drain and serve them. You may also want to try the dried variety; if so, follow the package instructions for cooking, chill, and use in salads as per directions.

Whenever you are planning a buffet menu, do not overlook the value of using one or more vegetable and bean salads. They add color and variety to any menu.

HEARTS OF ARTICHOKE SALAD

To vary this recipe, try preparing it with Curry Dressing (see index).

2 *packages frozen artichoke hearts, 10-ounce size, cooked according to package directions, drained and cooled*
1 *pint cherry tomatoes*
1 *small onion, chopped fine*
1 *small head iceberg lettuce, torn into small pieces*
½ *cup Basic French Dressing (see index)*

Lightly toss artichoke hearts, cherry tomatoes, onion, and lettuce together. Pour dressing over all, and toss lightly. Serve immediately.

Serves 6.

BROCCOLI SALAD

1 *pound fresh broccoli*
1 *tablespoon lemon juice*
½ *cup mayonnaise*
2 *tablespoons chopped onion*
½ *teaspoon salt*
   freshly ground pepper
2 *hard-boiled egg yolks*

Rinse broccoli, and trim off leaves. Chop into good-sized pieces, and drop into rapidly boiling salted water to cover vegetable; cook for about 8 minutes, until tender. The broccoli should be slightly crisp. Drain and cool. Mix lemon juice, mayonnaise, chopped onion, salt and pepper, then pour over broccoli. Lightly toss. Chill thoroughly. Just before serving, press egg yolks through strainer. Use them to garnish the salad.

Serves 6.

BROCCOLI AND CAULIFLOWER SALAD

This salad is lovely as an appetizer served with toast.

        1 *head broccoli*
        1 *head cauliflower*
        2 *hard-boiled eggs, chopped fine*
       ¾ *cup Vinaigrette Dressing (see index)*

Cut flowerets from broccoli and cauliflower, and cook them in rapidly boiling water for 8 minutes. Drain. Mix with hard-boiled eggs. Place into small ring mold and pour sauce over top. Press ingredients down, and chill for several hours.

Serves 6.

CUCUMBERS IN SOUR CREAM

        2 *cucumbers, peeled and thinly sliced*
        1 *medium-sized onion, thinly sliced*
        1 *tablespoon chopped chives*
       ⅔ *tablespoon cider vinegar*
        1 *tablespoon sugar*
       ¾ *cup sour cream*
          salt and pepper to taste

Combine cucumbers, onion, and chives in a bowl. Blend remaining ingredients, and pour over cucumber mixture. Chill thoroughly.

Serves 6.

RADISH AND CUCUMBER SALAD

        2 *cucumbers*
       12 *radishes*
       ½ *cup water*
       ¼ *cup wine vinegar*
        1 *teaspoon sugar*

½ *teaspoon salt*
   pepper to taste
¼ *cup olive oil*

Peel cucumbers, and slice thin. Trim off ends of radishes, and slice very thin. Place cucumbers and radishes in a bowl; add water, vinegar, sugar, salt and pepper. Cover, and refrigerate for at least 1 hour, but not more than 3. Add oil, and mix gently. Check seasoning.

Serves 6.

SAUERKRAUT SALAD

1 *can sauerkraut, 20-ounce size, rinsed and drained*
1 *medium onion, chopped fine*
1 *green pepper, chopped fine*
2 *tablespoons sugar*

Combine ingredients, and chill. Adjust seasoning to taste before serving.

Serves 4 to 6.

RED ONION AND ORANGE SALAD

4 *oranges*
2 *small red onions, sliced thin*
½ *cup Basic French Dressing (see index)*

Peel the oranges, carefully removing the skin and the white membrane. Cut the oranges into bite-sized pieces, and remove the seeds. Combine the oranges and onions, and chill until serving time. Just before serving, gently mix in the dressing. Arrange on crisp lettuce leaves, and serve.

Serves 4.

GREEN VEGETABLE SALAD

1 package baby lima beans, 10-ounce size, cooked, drained and cooled
2 cups cooked green beans, cut into 1-inch lengths, drained and cooled
1 cup cooked green peas, drained and cooled
1 tablespoon fresh chopped parsley
¼ cup chopped scallions
1 small green pepper, chopped fine
¼ cup mayonnaise
¼ cup Basic French Dressing (see index)

Combine lima beans, green beans, peas, parsley, scallions, and green pepper in large bowl. Blend mayonnaise and Basic French Dressing with wire whisk, and pour over salad. Toss and chill.

Serves 6 to 8.

BUTTON MUSHROOM SALAD

1 jar or can button mushrooms, 1-pound size, drained
4 scallions, minced
1 small green pepper, minced
2 shredded carrots
½ cup Garlic Dressing (see index)

Combine ingredients; cover, and refrigerate for 30 minutes before serving.

Serves 4.

MARINATED MUSHROOMS

1 pound fresh mushrooms, cleaned, trimmed and sliced
1 tablespoon fresh chopped parsley
3 scallions, minced
1 clove garlic, crushed
½ teaspoon dried thyme
¼ cup olive oil

2 *tablespoons lemon juice*
¼ *teaspoon salt*
  pepper to taste

Place mushrooms in a bowl with the parsley and scallions. In a small bowl, combine garlic, thyme, and salt and pepper. Mix in lemon juice. Slowly add olive oil. Pour dressing over mushrooms. Cover, and refrigerate for several hours before serving.

Serves 4 to 6.

COLD, MINTED GREEN BEAN SALAD

1 *pound green beans, cooked and cooled*
½ *cup olive oil*
3 *tablespoons wine vinegar*
¼ *teaspoon dry mustard*
1 *tablespoon chopped mint*
  or
1 *teaspoon dried mint*
  salt and pepper to taste

Place olive oil, vinegar, dry mustard, mint, salt and pepper to taste in a bowl, and whisk with wire whisk until well blended. Adjust seasoning. Cut string beans into 1-inch lengths, and pour dressing over beans. Chill for several hours.

Serves 4 to 6.

CARROT AND RAISIN SALAD

2 *cups grated carrots*
1 *cup raisins*
1 *cup chopped celery*
1 *cup diced apple*
⅓ *cup mayonnaise*
  pinch sugar
  salt and pepper to taste
  lettuce leaves for garnish

Combine dry ingredients and blend. Add mayonnaise, and stir to mix. Adjust seasoning to taste. Serve on crisp lettuce leaves.

Serves 4 to 6.

PEA AND CHEESE SALAD

 1 *can small green peas, 16-ounce size, drained*
 1 *onion, finely chopped*
 4 *ounces cheddar cheese, cubed*
 1 *hard-boiled egg, chopped*
 ¼ *cup mayonnaise*
 1 *teaspoon lemon juice*
   salt and pepper to taste

Combine green peas, onion, cheese, and egg. In a small bowl, blend mayonnaise and lemon juice. Stir into other ingredients, and season well with salt and pepper. Chill for several hours.

Serves 4 to 6.

COMBINATION VEGETABLE SALAD

 ½ *cup vegetable oil*
 1 *pound zucchini, quartered lengthwise and sliced in ¼-inch pieces*
 ½ *cup whole kernel corn*
 2 *stalks celery, chopped*
 1 *green pepper, chopped*
 6 *scallions, sliced thin*
 2 *tomatoes, peeled, seeded, and chopped*
 3 *tablespoons wine vinegar*
 1 *tablespoon dried basil*
 1 *teaspoon salt*
   fresh grated pepper

Heat oil in Dutch oven, and add all ingredients. Toss in pan gently; cover, and simmer for 5 minutes. Toss again, and cook 5 minutes more. Serve hot or cold.

Serves 6.

BASIC COLESLAW

4 *cups shredded cabbage*
1 *shredded carrot*
½ *green pepper, chopped*
1 *medium onion, chopped*
½ *teaspoon celery seeds*
½ *cup mayonnaise*
½ *teaspoon salt*
   pepper to taste

Combine cabbage, carrot, green pepper, onion, and celery seeds; mix. Add mayonnaise. Season to taste with salt and pepper.

Serves 6.

HELEN ABBOTT'S COLESLAW

2 *pounds finely shredded cabbage*
½ *cup mayonnaise*
2 *tablespoons Dijon mustard*
2 *tablespoons sugar*
2 *tablespoons honey*
2 *tablespoons vinegar*
4 *tablespoons heavy cream*
4 *tablespoons caraway seeds*
½ *teaspoon prepared horseradish*

Combine ingredients well, and chill for several hours before serving.

Serves 6 to 8.

APPLE COLESLAW

This variation on coleslaw is especially tasty during fall when apples are in full season.

        3 *cups shredded cabbage*
        2 *tart apples, cored but not peeled, then diced*
     ½ *cup raisins*
     ½ *cup mayonnaise*
        1 *tablespoon lemon juice*
           salt to taste

Toss ingredients well, and chill thoroughly.

Serves 6.

COLESLAW WITH SOUR CREAM DRESSING

     ½ *cup sour cream*
     ½ *cup mayonnaise*
        3 *tablespoons lemon juice*
     ¼ *cup minced scallions*
        1 *teaspoon prepared mustard*
        1 *teaspoon celery seed*
        1 *teaspoon sugar*
        1 *teaspoon salt*
           pepper to taste
        4 *cups shredded cabbage*
     ½ *cup raisins*

Combine ingredients except cabbage and raisins. Blend well. Pour over cabbage and raisins, and lightly toss until cabbage is evenly coated with dressing.

Serves 6 to 8.

LENTIL SALAD

        1 *cup dried lentils*
        3 *tablespoons butter*

½ *pound chopped mushrooms*
¼ *cup chopped shallots*
2 *tablespoons olive oil*
1 *teaspoon soy sauce*
¼ *teaspoon salt*
2 *hard-boiled eggs, chopped*

Put lentils in a saucepan with 1 quart of water and lightly salt. Bring to a boil; reduce heat to a simmer, and cook for about 45 minutes, until water is absorbed and lentils are tender. Add a little extra water, if necessary. Melt butter in skillet and sauté mushrooms and shallots until liquid is absorbed. Add to lentils. Add olive oil, soy sauce, salt, and hard-boiled eggs. Combine well. Serve hot or cold.

Serves 4 to 6.

BLACK-EYED PEA SALAD

1 *package frozen black-eyed peas, 10-ounce size*
2 *hard-boiled eggs, finely chopped*
6 *gherkins, minced*
½ *cup mayonnaise*
1 *small onion, minced*
2 *stalks celery, finely chopped*

Cook black-eyed peas according to package directions; drain and cool. Add remaining ingredients, and mix.

Serves 4.

BEAN AND TUNA SALAD

2 *cans tuna, 7-ounce size, drained*
2 *cans cannellini beans, 20-ounce size, drained*
1 *red onion, finely chopped*
1 *green pepper, diced*
1 *tablespoon fresh chopped parsley*
½ *cup olive oil*
¼ *cup wine vinegar*
  salt and pepper to taste

Combine tuna, cannellini beans, onion, and pepper. Sprinkle chopped parsley over top. Combine olive oil and vinegar, and pour over salad. Toss lightly. Season to taste.

Serves 6 to 8.

KIDNEY BEAN SALAD I

> 1 *can kidney beans, 16-ounce size, drained*
> 1 *medium-sized onion, minced*
> 1 *cup chopped celery*
> 1/3 *cup chopped sweet pickles*
> 2 *hard-boiled eggs, chopped*
> 1/2 *cup mayonnaise*
> 1/2 *teaspoon salt*
> *pepper to taste*

Combine kidney beans, onion, celery, pickles, and eggs. Gently fold in mayonnaise. Season to taste. Chill for a few hours.

Serves 4 to 6.

KIDNEY BEAN SALAD II

> 4 *cups drained, canned red kidney beans*
> 6 *scallions, finely sliced*
> 1 *clove garlic, crushed*
> 1 *green pepper, chopped*
> 1/2 *cup vegetable oil*
> 3 *tablespoons red wine vinegar*
> 1/4 *teaspoon dry mustard*
> 1/4 *teaspoon oregano*
> 1 *tablespoon fresh chopped parsley*
> 1/2 *teaspoon salt*

In a large bowl, place drained kidney beans, scallions, garlic, and green pepper; combine. In a separate bowl, beat together the vegetable oil, vinegar, mustard, oregano, parsley, and salt.

Pour over the salad mixture. Cover and refrigerate for several hours.

Serves 8.

KIDNEY BEAN AND CHEESE SALAD

1 *can kidney beans, 16-ounce size, drained*
6 *strips crisp cooked bacon, crumbled*
½ *cup chopped celery*
1 *small onion, chopped*
1 *cup diced cheddar cheese*
½ *cup mayonnaise*
½ *teaspoon salt*
  pepper to taste
  parsley (for garnish)

Combine kidney beans, bacon, celery, onion, and cheese; chill thoroughly. Gently fold in mayonnaise. Season to taste. Sprinkle with chopped parsley for garnish.

Serves 4 to 6.

WHITE KIDNEY BEAN SALAD

1 *can cannellini beans, 20-ounce size, drained*
¼ *cup minced scallions*
1 *clove garlic, crushed*
2 *tomatoes, peeled and chopped*
2 *stalks celery, finely chopped*
1 *tablespoon lemon juice*
½ *cup olive oil*
  salt and pepper to taste

Blend cannellini beans, scallions, garlic, tomatoes, and celery. Sprinkle with lemon juice. Pour olive oil over food. Season to taste, and chill thoroughly.

Serves 4.

BUTTER BEAN AND CORN SALAD

  1 *can butter beans, 16-ounce size, drained*
  1 *can corn, 8-ounce size*
  2 *pimientos, minced*
  1 *medium-sized onion, minced*
  1 *clove garlic, crushed (optional)*
 ½ *teaspoon Worcestershire sauce*
  3 *tablespoons vegetable oil*
  2 *tablespoons vinegar*

Combine butter beans, corn, pimientos, and onion gently. Mix garlic, Worcestershire sauce, vegetable oil, and vinegar; pour over salad. Serve immediately.

Serves 4.

MIXED BEAN SALAD

  1 *can red kidney beans, 20-ounce size, drained*
  1 *can cannellini beans, 20-ounce size, drained*
  1 *can chickpeas, 16-ounce size, drained*
  1 *medium-sized onion, finely chopped*
 ½ *teaspoon dried oregano*
 ½ *teaspoon dried basil*
 ½ *cup olive oil*
  2 *tablespoons red wine vinegar*
    salt and pepper to taste

Combine red kidney beans, cannellini beans, chickpeas and onions. Sprinkle on oregano and basil. In a small bowl, beat vinegar into olive oil. Drizzle over salad, and lightly toss to mix. Season to taste.

Serves 6 to 8.

CELERIAC SALAD

Celeriac, also called celery root, can be found in food shops throughout France, prepared as it is here. It is a good, light salad that goes with most main dishes.

2 *celeriac knobs*
¼ *cup olive oil*
½ *teaspoon prepared mustard*
2 *tablespoons lemon juice*
2 *tablespoons grated onion*
1 *tablespoon fresh chopped parsley*
  salt and pepper to taste
¼ *cup mayonnaise*

Clean and peel celeriac knobs; cut into large chunks. Place celeriac knobs in boiling salted water; cover and cook until tender, about 10-15 minutes. Drain and cool; cut into julienne strips. Transfer to a bowl. Combine olive oil, mustard, lemon juice, grated onion, salt and pepper to taste. Pour over celeriac, and mix gently. Cover and refrigerate overnight, stirring once or twice. Before serving, add mayonnaise, and toss lightly until well blended. Sprinkle with parsley.

Serves 4 to 6.

CARROT SALAD

Oddly enough, this simple salad pleases most palates. Men, women, and children heap large helpings of this delightful salad on their plates, so be prepared. For variation, add raisins, black olives, or chopped green pepper, or stuff hollowed-out ripe tomatoes (one per serving) with the carrot mixture.

⅓ *cup vegetable oil*
2 *tablespoons vinegar*
1 *tablespoon sugar*
4 *cups finely shredded carrots*
1 *tablespoon fresh chopped parsley*
  salt and pepper

Combine vegetable oil, vinegar, and sugar. Pour over carrots and add parsley. Season well with salt and pepper. Toss; cover, and chill.

Serves 6.

CALICO SALAD

This salad is delicious served in hollowed-out tomato shells. Use it as a side dish or as an appetizer.

> 3 *cups cooked rice, cooled*
> ½ *cup corn*
> ½ *cup chopped green pepper*
> ¼ *cup chopped pimiento*
> 1 *jar cocktail onions, 3½-ounce size, drained*
> ½ *cup pitted black olives, halved*
> ½ *cup Basic French Dressing (see index)*

Set three olives aside to be used as garnish. Place rice, corn, green pepper, pimiento, onions, and remaining olives in a large bowl. Blend in dressing. Garnish with olives. Chill well before serving.

Serves 6 to 8.

SAUERKRAUT RELISH SALAD

> 1 *can sauerkraut, 16-ounce size, drained*
> 1 *cup chopped celery*
> 1 *cup chopped green pepper*
> ½ *cup chopped onion*
> ½ *cup whole kernel corn*
> 2 *cups shredded carrots*
> 2 *pimientos, chopped*
> ⅔ *cup sugar*
> 3 *tablespoons white vinegar*
> 1 *teaspoon salt*
> *fresh ground pepper*

Combine ingredients in a bowl; cover and refrigerate for at least 6 hours.

Serves 8.

VEGETABLE SONG SALAD

To turn this dish into a stunning cold buffet dish or light supper, unmold on lettuce greens on very large platter, and garnish with rolled cold cuts and sliced cheese.

- 1 *package, 10-ounce size, mixed vegetables, cooked, drained, and cooled*
- ¼ *cup chopped green pepper*
- 1 *stalk celery, chopped*
- 2 *scallions, sliced thin*
- 1 *cucumber, peeled, seeded, and diced*
- ½ *cup cold water*
- 2 *packages unflavored gelatin*
- 1 *cup hot chicken broth*
- 2 *tablespoons fresh lemon juice*
- 1 *cup Thousand Island Dressing (see index)*

Combine the vegetables in large bowl. Soften the gelatin by putting it in small saucepan with cold water. Pour hot chicken broth over the gelatin and water, and simmer, stirring until gelatin dissolves. Stir in lemon juice and dressing, then pour over vegetables and combine. Chill until slightly thickened, and transfer into a 6-cup mold. Chill until firm.

Serves 6 to 8.

VEGETABLE BOWL

- 1 *head cauliflower, cut into small flowerets*
- 1 *pound fresh mushrooms, quartered*
- 1 *zucchini, diced*
- 1 *can peas, 8-ounce size, drained*
- ½ *cup crisp cooked crumbled bacon*
- 1 *small onion, chopped*
- ¾ *cup Vinaigrette Dressing (see index)*

Combine cauliflower, mushrooms, zucchini, and peas in a large bowl. Add bacon and onion. Toss lightly in dressing. Cover and refrigerate for 2 hours.

Serves 8.

FRESH VEGETABLES AND COTTAGE CHEESE

½ *cup chopped green pepper*
½ *cup chopped celery*
½ *cup chopped cucumber*
½ *cup shredded carrots*
1 *small onion, minced*
2 *cups cottage cheese*
1 *tablespoon Worcestershire sauce*
1 *teaspoon lemon juice*
   dash Tabasco sauce
   salt and pepper to taste

In a bowl, combine green pepper, celery, cucumber, carrots, and onion. Stir Worcestershire sauce and lemon juice into cottage cheese. Add Tabasco sauce, and season to taste. Blend gently into vegetables. Chill thoroughly before serving.

Serves 4.

Fruit Salads

There is no food quite as refreshing as a fresh fruit salad served with an appropriate dressing. Fruit salads are highly decorative and colorful as well as nutritious. They are popular as healthful meals these days, accompanied with cottage cheese or tasty sandwiches, and make delightful desserts.

Certain fruits, such as bananas, oranges and apples, are available all year long. When other fruits are needed but cannot be found fresh, investigate canned or dried fruit. Pineapple, peaches, apricots, and pears are always available canned. When combined with fresh fruit, a very good salad results. Dried fruits are particularly good with cottage cheese and nuts.

Creamy sweet salad dressings are wonderful with fruit salads, whether made with mayonnaise, yogurt, or sour cream. Garnishes are important to fruit salads. Sometimes a dab of dressing alone is just the right touch. Cherries are the old standby, but also try fresh mint leaves, watercress, chopped nuts, or raisins. Experiment to find your own favorite fruit salad combinations.

ENDIVE AND ORANGE SALAD

Salad:
4 *medium-sized endive*
2 *oranges*

Dressing:
⅓ *cup orange juice*
1 *tablespoon lemon juice*
1 *teaspoon grated orange rind*
3 *tablespoons olive oil*
1 *tablespoon soy sauce*
1 *clove garlic, crushed*

Discard outer leaves of endive, and cut off bottom. Slice each endive into sections about one inch long. Separate the leaves, and place in a bowl. Peel oranges, and cut away the white membrane around outside; then slice thin, and remove seeds. Transfer orange slices to the bowl with the endive. Mix dressing ingredients, and pour over salad. Gently toss.

Serves 4.

FRESH CHERRY SALAD

Serving suggestion: This is delicious with plain sponge or coffee cake.

1 *pound fresh cherries, pitted*
⅓ *cup mayonnaise*
1 *tablespoon fresh orange juice*
1 *package whole pecans, 2½-ounce size*

Combine ingredients gently and serve on crisp lettuce leaves.

Serves 4.

GRAPEFRUIT, ROMAINE, AND RED ONION SALAD

1 *head romaine lettuce*

2 grapefruits
1 red onion, sliced thin
⅓ cup vegetable oil
2 tablespoons vinegar
2 tablespoons grapefruit juice
2 tablespoons heavy cream
½ teaspoon sugar
¼ teaspoon salt
pepper to taste

Wash lettuce leaves, and pat dry. Tear into pieces, and place in salad bowl. Peel grapefruit; remove membrane, and place sections in bowl with lettuce and onions. While preparing grapefruit, reserve 2 tablespoons grapefruit juice. In a small bowl mix oil, vinegar, grapefruit juice, heavy cream, sugar, salt and pepper with a wire whisk. Pour dressing over salad.

Serves 4.

MELON SALAD

1 cantaloupe
1 honeydew melon
2 cups seeded watermelon balls
1 cup blueberries
½ cup vegetable oil
2 tablespoons lemon juice
1 tablespoon orange juice
½ teaspoon dried mint (optional)
salt and pepper

Remove seeds from cantaloupe and honeydew melon, and make balls with melon cutter. Place in a bowl with watermelon balls and blueberries. In a small bowl, add oil, lemon juice, orange juice, and dried mint. Season with salt and pepper. Beat well with a wire whisk, and pour over melon mixture. Toss gently and chill for 1 hour.

Serves 6.

FRUIT-FILLED CANTALOUPE

2 *cantaloupes*
2 *cups fresh blueberries*
2 *cups fresh strawberries*
1 *cup fresh pineapple chunks*
½ *cup port wine*
2 *tablespoons orange juice*
1 *tablespoon sugar*

Cut cantaloupes in half, and scoop out seeds. Wash and remove stems from blueberries and strawberries. Place blueberries, strawberries, and pineapple in large bowl. In another bowl, blend remaining ingredients, and pour over fruit. Toss. Spoon fruit and sauce in equal portions into cantaloupe halves.

Serves 4.

PLUM AND CANTALOUPE SALAD

6 *large plums, pitted and cut into wedges*
1 *large ripe cantaloupe*
½ *cup Lemon Dressing (see index)*

Cut cantaloupe and remove pulp. Cut into bite-sized pieces or make melon balls. Combine and gently toss ingredients. Serve on crisp lettuce greens.

Serves 4 to 6.

SUMMER FRUIT SALAD

2 *cups cantaloupe balls*
1 *cup blueberries*
1 *cup strawberries, halved*
1 *cup white seedless grapes*
3 *peaches, peeled, pitted, and cut into thin slices*
½ *cup Fruit Salad Dressing (see index)*

Mix ingredients in large bowl, and lightly toss until fruit is well coated.

Serves 6.

FOR-THE-LADIES-WHO-LUNCH SALAD

6 *canned pear halves*
3 *ounces cream cheese*
2 *tablespoons orange juice*
1 *tablespoon rum*
 good dash ginger
⅔ *cup toasted almond slivers*
 curly endive

Cream together cream cheese, orange juice, rum, and ginger. Spread mixture on back of pear halves which have been patted dry with paper towels. Stick almond slivers into each coated pear, forming a prickly effect, and place in individual salad plates lined with curly endive.

Serves 6.

WALDORF SALAD

1 *large apple, cored and diced*
1 *large pear, cored and diced*
1 *cup seedless white grapes*
½ *cup chopped celery*
½ *cup chopped walnuts*
⅓ *cup mayonnaise*
1 *tablespoon lemon juice*
½ *teaspoon sugar*
¼ *teaspoon ginger*

Place apple, pear, grapes, celery, and walnuts in bowl. Combine remaining ingredients, and pour over salad. Toss lightly until evenly coated, and chill thoroughly.

Serves 4.

GINGER PEACH SALAD

1 *head Bibb lettuce*
4 *large, ripe peaches*
⅓ *cup vegetable oil*
   juice of 1 lemon
½ *teaspoon ground ginger*
½ *teaspoon sugar*

Wash and dry lettuce; tear into pieces, and place in salad bowl. Peel, pit, and slice the peaches. Toss them with remaining ingredients, and turn onto lettuce. Serve immediately.

Serves 4.

CAMEMBERT AND PEAR SALAD

1 *head Bibb lettuce*
6 *ounces Camembert cheese, cubed*
2 *ripe pears, cored, peeled and cubed*
⅓ *cup Basic French Dressing (see index)*

Wash and dry lettuce; tear into pieces. Toss ingredients gently and serve.

Serves 4.

FRESH PINEAPPLE SALAD

1 *head iceberg lettuce*
1 *ripe pineapple, peeled, cored and cut into 1-inch thick slices*
½ *cup mayonnaise*
1 *large ripe avocado, cut into 1-inch balls*
   juice of 1 lemon
¾ *cup grated American cheese*

Arrange crisp lettuce leaves on four individual plates. Place a slice of pineapple on each, then spoon mayonnaise in equal amounts into holes in pineapple. Lightly toss avocado balls in lemon juice, and arrange them on top of mayonnaise on each pineapple. Finally, sprinkle grated cheese over salads, and serve immediately.

Serves 4.

BANANA SALAD

5 *ripe bananas*
1 *cup plain yogurt*
1 *teaspoon lemon juice*
3 *tablespoons honey*
1 *tablespoon rum*
2 *cups cottage cheese*
2 *cups cantaloupe balls*
2 *cups strawberries*
½ *cup chopped pecans*

To make dressing, place 1 sliced banana in a blender with yogurt, lemon juice, honey, and rum. Blend until smooth, or mash banana with fork to blend well with ingredients. To assemble salad, slice 1 banana, topped with a scoop of cottage cheese, into four individual serving dishes. Surround equally with cantaloupe balls and strawberries. Spoon dressing over salad, and sprinkle with pecans.

Serves 4.

WATERCRESS AND APRICOT SALAD

1 *bunch watercress*
1 *pound fresh apricots*
½ *cup Fruit Salad Dressing (see index)*

Clean the watercress, removing stems. Peel the apricots; cut into quarters, and remove their pits. Put the apricots and watercress in a bowl, and pour on the dressing.

Serves 4 to 6.

FRUIT COMPOTE WITH YOGURT TOPPING

1 *cup plain yogurt*
1 *ripe banana, sliced*
2 *tablespoons honey*
1 *apple, peeled, cored, and sliced*
1 *orange, peeled, seeded, and cut into sections*
1 *cup seedless green grapes*
1 *cup strawberries, halved*

To make dressing, place yogurt, banana, and honey in blender; cover, and purée until smooth. Place remaining fruits in a glass bowl, and spoon dressing over the top.

Serves 4.

1940s KANSAS FRUIT SALAD

This salad gained great popularity throughout the Midwest during the forties, and is still a regular feature of many Sunday dinner menus.

1 *package black cherry Jell-O*
½ *cup drained canned fruit cocktail (reserve liquid)*
1 *banana, sliced*
½ *cup purple grapes, halved and seeded*

Dissolve Jell-O in 1 cup of boiling water. Use the drained liquid from the canned fruit cocktail plus enough cold water to make 1 cup liquid. Add to Jell-O, and chill until slightly thickened. Fold in the remaining ingredients, and turn into a 4-cup mold. Chill until set.

Serves 6.

PINEAPPLE CRANBERRY SALAD

This salad is delicious topped with Orange Mayonnaise Dressing. It is an interesting variation on the traditional Thanksgiving cranberry salad.

1 *16-ounce can crushed pineapple*
1 *16-ounce can whole cranberry sauce*
½ *pint sour cream*
2 *packages plain gelatin*
½ *cup cold water*

Place pineapple, cranberry sauce, and sour cream in a bowl, and blend. Put gelatin in a small saucepan, and add cold water to soften it. Stir gelatin under low heat until dissolved. Pour gelatin into the salad mixture and combine. Turn into a 1-quart mold, and chill until set.

Serves 6.

FRESH PEAR SALAD
WITH BLUE CHEESE DRESSING

½ *cup vegetable oil*
2 *tablespoons lemon juice*
½ *teaspoon salt*
¼ *teaspoon dry mustard*
1 *teaspoon sugar*
  pepper to taste
2 *tablespoons crumbled blue cheese*
1 *head escarole, torn into small pieces*
4 *pears, peeled, cored and sliced*

Combine oil, lemon juice, salt, mustard, sugar, pepper, and blue cheese in a bowl, and beat with wire whisk. Place lettuce and sliced pears in salad bowl; pour blue cheese dressing over salad, and toss.

Serves 6.

Molded Salads

Molded salads are beautiful on the dining table, and have many advantages, too. A busy host or hostess can prepare a mold in advance. Salad molds are also quite inexpensive, and women, men, and children love them.

Try to build a collection of containers, such as melon and ring molds, and a wide variety of the fancy molds for fish and fruit. You don't have to go out and buy one for $25; there are inexpensive aluminum molds, and a simple loaf pan or baking tin can always be substituted. Individual molds take less time to set, and are extremely attractive. Substitute muffin tins for individual salad molds, if you don't want to make the special investment.

Here are a few general suggestions that are helpful when preparing molds:

(1) Do not use more gelatin than called for in a recipe,

because the mold will certainly be rubbery and the taste unpleasant.

(2) When a recipe tells you to "chill mold until slightly set," it means until the texture of the liquid has a syrupy consistency. Then it is ready for the folding in of remaining ingredients. If you don't wait until the gelatin is ready, the solid ingredients will rise to the top, instead of blending evenly into the mold.

(3) Fill a mold right up to the top so the shape will be pleasing. Always use the size container called for in a recipe.

(4) To unmold gelatin dishes, dip the mold or container into warm water to within ½ inch of its top for 5 seconds. Carefully loosen the edges of the mold from the side of the container with the tip of a spoon or a knife. Place a serving dish against the top of the mold; hold them together and turn them right side up. Gripping firmly, give the dish one good shake. If the dish does not unmold, repeat the process.

CRABMEAT SALAD MOLD

1 *package lemon Jell-O*
1½ *cups boiling water*
3 *tablespoons vinegar*
1 *cup finely chopped celery*
1 *small onion, grated*
1 *pimiento, minced*
2 *cups crabmeat*
½ *cup mayonnaise*

Dissolve the gelatin in boiling water, and add vinegar. Chill until mixture begins to set. Add celery, onion, pimiento, and crabmeat. Blend. Fold in mayonnaise, and pour into 6-cup mold. Chill until firm.

Serves 6.

NANCY DUSSAULT'S CORNED BEEF SALAD

Salad:
1 *package lemon Jell-O*
1 *teaspoon lemon juice*
1½ *cups hot water*
1 *can corned beef*
1½ *cups finely chopped celery*
2 *tablespoons chopped onion*
3 *hard-boiled eggs, chopped*
1 *cup mayonnaise*

Dressing:
½ *cup sour cream*
1 *teaspoon chives*

Heat water, and add Jell-O and lemon juice. Cool slightly. In a large bowl, add canned corned beef, celery, onion, chopped egg, and mayonnaise. Mix well; add lemon Jell-O and water mixture, and blend. Refrigerate until firm. Serve with dressing of combined sour cream and chives.

Serves 4 to 6.

CUCUMBER MOUSSE

3 *cucumbers*
1 *tablespoon lemon juice*
½ *teaspoon salt*
1 *teaspoon Worcestershire sauce*
½ *cup mayonnaise*
2 *envelopes unflavored gelatin*
3 *tablespoons cool water*
3 *tablespoons hot water*
1 *cup heavy cream, whipped*

Peel two cucumbers, and chop. Place the cucumbers in a blender with lemon juice, salt, Worcestershire sauce, and mayonnaise. Blend until smooth. Soften the gelatin in 3 tablespoons cool water, and then add 3 tablespoons hot water to dissolve. Add to the cucumber mixture, and fold in the whipped cream. Pour into a 1-quart mold, and chill until firm. Unmold mousse. Slice the remaining cucumber, and arrange it on top of the mousse.

Serves 6.

PIQUANT TOMATO ASPIC

2 *packages lemon Jell-O*
2½ *cups boiling water*
2 *cans tomato sauce, 8-ounce size*
1 *tablespoon lemon juice*
3 *tablespoons vinegar*
2 *teaspoons Worcestershire sauce*
½ *teaspoon salt*
  dash Tabasco sauce
1 *cup chopped stuffed green olives*
½ *cup chopped raw cauliflower*
½ *cup sliced scallions*
½ *cup black olive slivers*

Dissolve the Jell-O in boiling water, and remove from the heat. Add tomato sauce, lemon juice, vinegar, Worcestershire sauce, salt, and Tabasco sauce. Refrigerate until partially set; stir in remaining ingredients, and pour into a 2-quart mold. Refrigerate overnight.

Serves 8.

SWEET AND TANGY TOMATO ASPIC

½ cup water
1 package lemon Jell-O
2 cups tomato juice
1 tablespoon grated onion
2 teaspoons Worcestershire sauce
2 teaspoons vinegar
  dash Tabasco sauce

Bring ½ cup water to a boil, and dissolve the Jell-O in it. Add remaining ingredients. Pour into individual molds, and chill until firm.

Serves 4.

RICH PEACH MOLD

1 can peach halves, 20-ounce size
1 package orange Jell-O
1 package cream cheese, 3-ounce size
⅓ cup peach brandy or Grand Marnier
½ cup toasted almond slivers

Reserve the juice from the can of peaches, and add enough water to make 1⅔ cups liquid. Heat the combined peach liquid and water, and dissolve Jell-O in it. Add the cream cheese and liquor, and place in a blender. Blend for 15 seconds, until smooth. Pour into a 1-quart mold, and refrigerate until firm. Serve on a dish surrounded by lettuce, and sprinkle mold with almonds.

Serves 6.

COCONUT AND ORANGE MOLD

2 *packages orange Jell-O*
1¾ *cups hot water*
2 *cups canned pineapple juice*
2 *cups crushed pineapple*
1 *cup sour cream*
1 *can coconut, 8-ounce size*
1 *can mandarin oranges, 8-ounce size, drained*

Dissolve orange gelatin in water, and add pineapple juice, pineapple, sour cream, and coconut. Pour into a 2-quart mold, and chill until firm. Unmold, and cover top of mold with mandarin oranges.

Serves 8 to 10.

CHERRY WINE MOLD

2 *cans pitted dark sweet cherries, 16-ounce size, drained*
  with liquid reserved
2 *envelopes unflavored gelatin*
2 *teaspoons grated orange rind*
2 *tablespoons lemon juice*
1 *tablespoon sugar*
¼ *cup chopped chutney*
1 *cup dry red wine*
  mayonnaise

Heat liquid drained from canned cherries, and dissolve gelatin in it. Add orange rind, lemon juice, sugar, chutney, and red wine. Bring to a boil, and remove. Cool; add cherries, and pour into a 6-cup mold. Chill until firm. Serve with mayonnaise.

Serves 6 to 8.

BLUEBERRY AND CRANBERRY MOLD

2 *packages raspberry Jell-O*

2 *cups boiling water*
1 *pint blueberries, cleaned*
2 *cups cranberry juice*
1 *tablespoon lemon juice*
  sour cream

Dissolve raspberry gelatin in boiling water, and add blueberries, cranberry juice, and lemon juice. Pour into 6-cup mold, and chill until firm. Serve with sour cream.

Serves 6 to 8.

BLACK CHERRY SALAD WITH PORT

1 *package black cherry Jell-O*
1 *cup boiling water*
1 *cup port wine*
1 *can pitted bing cherries, 16-ounce size, drained*

Empty gelatin into a bowl, and pour boiling water over it. Stir until dissolved. Add wine, and chill until slightly jelled. Add cherries, and pour into a 1-quart mold. Refrigerate until firm, and serve on bed of crisp lettuce leaves with sour cream.

Serves 6.

NORMA'S SPECIAL SALAD MOLD

1 *package lime Jell-O*
½ *cup warm water*
1 *cup crushed pineapple*
½ *cup sugar*
  juice of 1 lemon
1 *cup shredded American cheese*
1 *cup pecans*
1 *cup mayonnaise*
1 *cup heavy cream, whipped*

Soak lime Jell-O in warm water for 5 minutes. In a saucepan, mix pineapple, sugar, and juice of lemon. Cook over low heat for 5 minutes. Pour pineapple mixture over Jell-O, and stir. Chill until Jell-O starts to set. Fold in remaining ingredients, and pour into 2-quart mold. Chill until firm.

Serves 6 to 8.

PEAR SALAD SUZANNE

Try this as a dessert with a teaspoon of creme de menthe on each serving.

    1 *package lime Jell-O*
      water
    1 *package cream cheese, 3-ounce size, room temperature*
    1 *can pears, 16-ounce size*
    1 *tablespoon lemon juice*
    ½ *pint heavy cream, whipped*

Drain and reserve the liquid from the can of pears. Prepare Jell-O according to package directions, using liquid from the canned pears, lemon juice, and enough water to make two cups of liquid. Chill Jell-O until it begins to jell, but is still soft. At this point, purée pears in a blender with cream cheese, or force pears through a food mill, and blend with cream cheese until smooth. Combine pear-cream cheese mixture with the soft lime Jell-O and fold in the whipped cream. Refrigerate until firm.

Serves 4 to 6.

PINEAPPLE LIME MOLD

    2 *envelopes unflavored gelatin*
      water
    ½ *cup lime juice*
    1 *can pineapple tidbits, 14-ounce size, liquid reserved*
    2 *teaspoons grated lime rind*

½ cup sugar
¼ teaspoon salt
1 cup orange juice
½ cup light rum
1 avocado, cubed

Soften gelatin in lime juice. Add enough water to liquid drained from pineapple tidbits to make two cups, and add lime rind, sugar, and salt. Heat until sugar is dissolved, stirring constantly. Add softened gelatin, and stir until thoroughly combined. Remove from the heat, and cool. Stir in the orange juice and rum. Refrigerate until mixture begins to set. Next, fold in avocado cubes and pineapple tidbits, and turn into 1½-quart mold. Chill until firm.

Serves 6 to 8.

LEMON TUNA SALAD MOLD

1 package lemon Jell-O
1 cup boiling water
1 teaspoon lemon juice
¾ cup cold water
1 7-ounce can tuna, drained and flaked
½ cup chopped celery
2 hard-boiled eggs, chopped
1 dill pickle, chopped
¼ cup chopped black olives
lettuce greens (garnish)

Dissolve Jell-O in boiling water. Add lemon juice and cold water. Chill until slightly thickened. Fold in remaining ingredients and turn into a loaf pan. Chill until firm. Unmold on lettuce greens, and decorate with cherry tomatoes, carrot curls, and green pepper strips, if desired.

Serves 4.

CRANBERRY SALAD MOLD

1 *package black cherry Jell-O*
½ *cup boiling water*
1 *can whole cranberry sauce, 16-ounce size*
1 *package cream cheese, 3-ounce size, at room temperature*
1 *can crushed pineapple, 8-ounce size, drained*
½ *cup chopped celery*
1 *cup chopped walnuts*

Dissolve Jell-O in boiling water, and slightly thicken in refrigerator. Fold in remaining ingredients, and turn into 6-cup mold. Chill until firm.

Serves 6 to 8.

COTTAGE CHEESE MOLD

1 *package unflavored gelatin*
¼ *cup canned pineapple juice*
2 *cups cottage cheese*
2 *cups strawberries*
   lettuce greens

Soften gelatin in pineapple juice in a small pan for a few minutes. Heat and stir until dissolved. Pour into blender; add cottage cheese and strawberries. Blend until smooth. Pour into a 1-quart mold, and chill until firm. Unmold on lettuce greens.

Serves 6.

AVOCADO MOUSSE

2 *envelopes unflavored gelatin*
2 *cups chicken broth*
2 *tablespoons lemon juice*
4 *scallions, finely sliced*
2 *large, ripe avocados*
½ *cup mayonnaise*

1 *teaspoon salt*
dash *Tabasco sauce*
1 *cup heavy cream, whipped*

Put 1 cup chicken broth in a small saucepan, and sprinkle gelatin over broth. Allow gelatin to soften for a minute or two, then heat, stirring until gelatin dissolves. Add remaining cup of broth, lemon juice, and scallions. Refrigerate until syrupy. Mash avocados until smooth and fold into gelatin mixture, along with mayonnaise, salt, and Tabasco. Finally, fold in whipped cream; adjust seasoning, and turn into a 6-cup mold. Chill until firm.

Serves 6 to 8.

Potato, Pasta and Rice Salads

This category of salads is a winner all around. Tasty, economical, and hearty, they make marvelous meals or side dishes. Potato salads, easy to prepare, are always family favorites. Famous at picnics, they are equally successful at indoor dinners.

Pasta salads make great main courses. Unfortunately too many cooks think only of macaroni when they consider pasta salads. Shells, ziti, and ditali are excellent pasta for use in salads, but most others can be used, too.

Be careful not to overcook whatever pasta you select, and you are bound to have an excellent tasty dish.

Rice is another food you may not have considered salad fare. It is well suited to chicken, seafood, cheese, vegetables—just about everything. The rice should be cooled before combining with other ingredients so it does not become mushy. Rice and vegetable salads are excellent with light vinaigrette dressings; rice and meat combinations often take a heavier dressing.

ZITI SALAD

Cold ziti salad is a nice change for a picnic when regular salads seem ordinary. It can be made a day in advance, so no last minute work is necessary.

1 *package, 16-ounce size, ziti macaroni*
1 *pound ground beef*
1 *medium-large onion, chopped*
1 *clove garlic, crushed*
1 *small green pepper, chopped*
1 *small red pepper, chopped*
1 *tablespoon finely chopped red (hot) pepper*
½ *cup olive oil*
2 *tablespoons red wine vinegar*
½ *teaspoon oregano*
½ *teaspoon salt*
   pepper to taste
1 *can whole kernel corn, 12-ounce size, drained*

Cook ziti according to package directions, and drain. Meanwhile, sauté beef with onion, garlic, and three peppers until meat is no longer pink and peppers are tender. Beat together oil, red wine vinegar, oregano, salt and pepper, and pour over drained ziti; add corn, and mix well, but gently. Cover and refrigerate until ready to serve.

Serves 6 to 8.

PLAIN AMERICAN POTATO SALAD

6 *medium-sized potatoes, cooked, peeled, and cubed*
2 *hard-boiled eggs, chopped*
1 *medium-sized onion, chopped*
1 *small green pepper, chopped fine*
½ *cup chopped celery*
½ *cup mayonnaise*
3 *tablespoons vinegar*
1 *teaspoon prepared mustard*
½ *teaspoon salt*
   pepper to taste

Place potatoes, eggs, onion, green pepper, and celery in a bowl, and lightly combine. Blend mayonnaise, vinegar, and mustard with salt and pepper. Pour over salad and gently blend. Chill for a few hours.

Serves 4 to 6.

GERMAN POTATO SALAD

 6 *medium-sized potatoes, cooked, peeled, and cut into thin slices*
 2 *hard-boiled eggs, chopped*
 8 *crisp, cooked bacon strips, crumbled (reserve 2 tablespoons bacon drippings)*
 6 *scallions, minced*
 ½ *cup chopped dill*
 1 *teaspoon celery seeds*
 ½ *teaspoon salt*
   pepper to taste
 ½ *cup vinegar*

Place hot, sliced potatoes in a large bowl with eggs, bacon, scallions, dill, celery seeds, and bacon drippings. Add salt and pepper, and lightly toss. Add vinegar, and toss again. Serve hot, or chill for several hours.

Serves 6.

POTATO AND SOUR CREAM SALAD

 6 *medium-sized potatoes, peeled, cooked, and cubed*
 2 *hard-boiled eggs*
 ⅓ *cup chopped scallions*
 1 *teaspoon celery seeds*
 1 *teaspoon salt*
   pepper to taste
 ¾ *cup sour cream*
 ¼ *cup mayonnaise*
 2 *tablespoons vinegar*
 1 *teaspoon prepared mustard*

Cut the eggs in half; chop the whites, and place the yolks in a small bowl. Place potatoes, egg whites, scallions, celery seeds, salt and pepper in a large bowl, and combine. Add the sour cream, mayonnaise, vinegar, and mustard to the egg yolks. Pour over the salad ingredients. Gently combine and chill for at least 1 hour.

Serves 6.

FRENCH POTATO SALAD

2 *pounds potatoes*
3 *stalks celery, chopped fine*
½ *cup minced scallions*
4 *ounces ham, cut into julienne strips*
1 *tablespoon chopped capers*
½ *teaspoon caper juice from bottle*
1 *tablespoon lemon juice*
1 *teaspoon Dijon mustard*
½ *cup heavy cream*
1 *teaspoon salt*
pepper to taste

Boil the potatoes in their skins. Remove from the water, and cool. Cut the potatoes into large cubes, and place in a large bowl. Add the remaining ingredients, and toss carefully. Adjust seasoning.

Serves 4 to 6.

DILLED POTATO SALAD

6 *potatoes, boiled, peeled, and diced*
1 *cup chopped celery*
1 *green pepper, finely chopped*
¼ *cup wine vinegar*
3 *tablespoons vegetable oil*
½ *teaspoon dry dill weed*
½ *teaspoon seasoned salt*
½ *cup sour cream*

Combine ingredients gently, and chill for several hours.

Serves 6.

SUMMER MACARONI SALAD

For variety, add 7 ounces tuna or 8 ounces ham cut into julienne strips. Or add 1 cup shredded American or cheddar cheese.

1 *pound elbow macaroni*
1 *medium-sized onion, chopped*
1 *cup chopped celery*
1 *small green pepper, chopped*
1 *large tomato, peeled and diced*
1 *teaspoon fresh, chopped parsley*
½ *teaspoon oregano*
1 *teaspoon salt*
¾ *cup mayonnaise*
1 *tablespoon lemon juice*

Cook the macaroni according to package directions. Drain and cool. Place in a large bowl, and add remaining ingredients. Blend, and chill thoroughly.

Serves 6 to 8.

ITALIAN CHICKEN SALAD

1 *cup uncooked ditali (macaroni)*
2 *medium-sized chicken breasts*
1 *bay leaf*
4 *peppercorns*
3 *stalks chopped celery*
 salt and pepper
½ *cup mayonnaise*
1 *tablespoon chopped capers*
2 *pimientos, chopped*
1 *teaspoon lemon juice*
1 *can sliced mushrooms, 8-ounce size, drained*
1 *medium-sized onion, minced*
½ *teaspoon basil*
¼ *teaspoon oregano*
½ *teaspoon salt*

Cook ditali according to package directions. Drain and cool.

Cover chicken breasts with water, and add bay leaf, pepper-corns, one stalk of chopped celery, and salt and pepper. Boil, covered, for 20 minutes. Remove chicken from cooking liquid, and cool. When cool enough to handle with your hands, remove the skin and bones from the chicken, and cut into cubes. Put it into a large bowl with the cooked macaroni, and add the remaining celery and all other ingredients. Blend with a spoon; check seasoning, and chill for several hours.

Serves 4 for lunch or 6 to 8 as side dish.

ITALIAN HAM SALAD

8 *ounces macaroni shells*
4 *ounces sliced, boiled ham, cut into strips 1½ by ½ inches*
½ *cup black olives, cut into slivers*
1 *ripe, firm tomato, diced*
1 *small green pepper, chopped*
1 *medium-sized onion, chopped*
½ *teaspoon dried basil*
½ *cup mayonnaise*
2 *tablespoons vinegar*
   salt and pepper

Cook macaroni shells according to package directions; drain and transfer to large bowl. Add ham, olives, tomato, green pepper, onion, and basil. Combine. Blend mayonnaise and vinegar; pour over salad, and gently toss. Season well with salt and pepper.

Serves 6 to 8.

CURRIED SHRIMP-RICE SALAD

2½ *cups cooked rice, cooled*
1 *can tiny Danish shrimp, 8-ounce size*
¼ *cup minced scallions*
1 *tablespoon chopped parsley*
1 *medium-sized green pepper, finely chopped*

1 *Delicious apple, cored and diced*
½ *cup raisins*
1 *pimiento, chopped fine*
⅓ *cup olive oil*
2 *tablespoons lemon juice*
1 *clove garlic, crushed*
1 *teaspoon curry powder*
½ *teaspoon sugar*
  salt and pepper to taste
  cherry tomatoes
  lettuce leaves for garnish

Combine rice, shrimp, scallions, parsley, green pepper, apple, raisins, and pimiento. In a separate bowl, blend together the remaining ingredients, except tomatoes, and pour over the rice mixture. Toss. Chill thoroughly. Line a serving dish with crisp lettuce leaves, and pile salad in the middle of the dish. Halve enough cherry tomatoes to make a border at edge of salad.

Serves 4.

RICE SALAD WITH VEGETABLES

3 *cups cooked rice, cooled*
3 *tablespoons vegetable oil*
2 *tablespoons wine vinegar*
1 *tablespoon prepared mustard*
½ *teaspoon salt*
  pepper to taste
1 *package frozen mixed vegetables, 10-ounce size*
1 *small green pepper, diced*
3 *scallions, sliced*

Cook frozen vegetables according to package directions; drain and cool. Place oil, vinegar, mustard, salt and pepper in a small bowl, and whisk until blended. Place the remaining ingredients in a large bowl; pour the dressing over them, and toss. Chill.

Serves 6.

SALAD VAN GOGH

To show off the pretty color of the salad, serve it in a large glass bowl.

1 *head romaine lettuce*
1 *cup cubed boiled potatoes*
2 *tomatoes, peeled and cut into wedges*
3 *scallions, sliced thin*
4 *strips crisply cooked bacon, crumbled*
2 *tablespoons freshly grated Parmesan cheese*
1 *cup croutons*
½ *cup Fines Herbes Dressing (see index)*

Combine lettuce, potatoes, tomatoes, scallions, and bacon in a salad bowl. Sprinkle with Parmesan cheese. Toss lightly, add crôutons and dressing. Toss and serve immediately.

Serves 4.

POTATO SALAD WITH BOILED DRESSING

6 *medium-sized potatoes*
¼ *cup wine vinegar*
1 *medium onion, chopped*
3 *stalks celery, chopped*
1 *teaspoon salt*
 freshly ground pepper
½ *cup vegetable oil*
3 *tablespoons wine vinegar*
1 *tablespoon flour*
¼ *teaspoon dry mustard*
½ *teaspoon sugar*
¼ *teaspoon salt*
2 *egg yolks*

Cook potatoes; peel and slice when cool enough to handle. Place in large bowl with ¼ cup wine vinegar, onion, celery, salt and pepper. Toss lightly. Cover and refrigerate until an hour before serving. In a double boiler, whisk together oil, vinegar, flour, mustard, sugar, and salt. When the water in the double boiler is hot, add the egg yolks, heating until sauce thickens. Cool and pour over potato salad. Combine, and let set at room temperature until ready to serve.

Serves 6.

SWEET POTATO SALAD

  2 *cups diced, cooked sweet potatoes*
  1 *cup diced, cooked ham*
  3 *tablespoons gherkin pickles, chopped*
  ¼ *cup sour cream*
  2 *tablespoons honey*

Place sweet potatoes, ham, and pickles in a bowl. Mix the sour cream and honey together, and blend gently with the sweet potato mixture. Chill well.

Serves 4 to 6.

Diet Salads

With a judicious choice and use of ingredients and dressings, salads can be a dieter's best friend. Low calorie vegetables that are perfect in salads include greens, carrots, celery, tomatoes, green peppers, cucumbers, asparagus, and radishes. Use as little oil, mayonnaise, or cream in your dressing as possible.

DIET SALAD BOWL

1 *pound leaf spinach, cleaned, trimmed, and torn into pieces*
3 *shredded carrots*
2 *stalks celery, chopped*
6 *sliced radishes*
6 *scallions, sliced*
1 *small cucumber, peeled and diced*
½ *cup Diet Herb Dressing (see index)*

Toss spinach, carrots, celery, radishes, scallions, and cucumbers together in a salad bowl. Pour dressing on salad, and toss.

Serves 6.

SHRIMP AND BEAN SPROUT SALAD

½ *pound chopped, boiled shrimp*
2 *cups bean sprouts, drained*
1 *can button mushrooms, 2-ounce size, drained*
¼ *cup chopped scallions*
1 *clove garlic, crushed*
¼ *cup peanut oil*
2 *tablespoons soy sauce*
2 *tablespoons vinegar*
   salt and pepper to taste

Toss ingredients together, and chill well. Serve on lettuce leaves or use as stuffing in several scooped-out tomatoes.

Serves 4.

EASY BEET AND ORANGE SALAD

1 *can sliced beets, 16-ounce size, drained*
½ *cup orange juice*
1 *tablespoon grated orange rind*
½ *teaspoon prepared mustard*

Place the beets in a bowl, and combine remaining ingredients.

Pour over beets, and lightly toss. Serve on crisp lettuce greens.

Serves 4.

YOGURT AND CUCUMBER SALAD

This delicious salad couldn't be easier to prepare, and it's always a winner.

> 1 *cup plain yogurt*
> 1 *large cucumber, peeled and sliced*
> 1 *large garlic clove, crushed*
> ¼ *teaspoon celery salt*
> *salt and pepper to taste*

Combine ingredients; cover, and refrigerate for 30 minutes. Stir ingredients before serving.

Serves 4.

TOMATO ASPIC WITH CHICKEN

> 2 *envelopes unflavored gelatin*
> 4 *cups tomato juice*
> 1 *teaspoon Worcestershire sauce*
> ½ *teaspoon celery salt*
> ½ *teaspoon chopped parsley*
> ½ *teaspoon sugar*
> 2 *cups cubed, cooked chicken*
> *lettuce for garnish*

Soften gelatin in ¼ cup cold water. Meanwhile, heat tomato juice and stir in softened gelatin until dissolved. Add Worcestershire sauce, celery salt, parsley, and sugar. Chill until slightly thickened, and fold in chicken. Pour into a 6-cup ring mold, and chill until firm. Unmold on lettuce greens.

Serves 6.

DIET SPINACH MOLD

   1 *package, 10-ounce size, frozen, chopped spinach*
1½ *cups hot spinach liquid and chicken broth*
   1 *package unflavored gelatin*
   1 *teaspoon grated onion*
   1 *tablespoon lemon juice*
  ¼ *teaspoon salt*
     fresh pepper to taste

Cook spinach according to package directions. Drain spinach and reserve liquid and add enough chicken broth to it to make 1½ cups. Soften gelatin in ¼ cup warm water in small pan for two minutes. Heat until dissolved and stir into hot chicken broth mixture. Add spinach. Add remaining ingredients, then turn into quart mold. Chill until firm.

Serves 4.

Sandwich Salads

The sandwich is probably America's favorite lunch. Tuna salad might well be the most popular sandwich in this country, and two tasty stand-bys are included in this chapter. Sandwich saladmaking offers an opportunity to do some experimenting with leftover chicken, beef, or veal. A dab of mayonnaise, scallions or onions, lemon juice, and freshly ground peppercorns can do wonders for what goes between two slices of bread. Try different herbs and spices, too. Curried tuna, for example, is a surprisingly different sandwich filling. For garnish, add lettuce greens, tomatoes or pickles.

Best of all, use a variety of breads such as French rolls, English muffins, rye, or pumpernickel.

ZESTY TUNA AND EGG SALAD

To vary this dish, scoop out two tomatoes; mix the tomato pulp into salad, then fill tomato hollows with tuna salad.

1 *can tuna, 7-ounce size, drained*
3 *hard-boiled eggs, chopped*
½ *cup mayonnaise or as needed*
½ *teaspoon celery seeds*
3 *scallions, minced*
  healthy dash of Tabasco sauce
  salt and pepper to taste

Place tuna, eggs, celery seeds, and scallions, in a large bowl. Add mayonnaise, Tabasco sauce, and salt and pepper to taste. Fold in gently to mix.

Makes 2 to 3 sandwiches or 2 salads.

REGULAR TUNA SALAD

This recipe makes two healthy-sized sandwiches or serves as salad for two accompanied by slices of cucumber, tomato, and green pepper.

1 *can tuna, 7-ounce size, drained*
½ *cup mayonnaise*
2 *stalks celery, minced*
2 *tablespoons minced onion*
1 *teaspoon lemon juice*
1 *teaspoon chopped parsley*
  salt and pepper to taste

Blend ingredients well with a fork.

Makes 2 large sandwiches or serves 2 as salad.

CRABMEAT SANDWICH SALAD

1 *pound crabmeat*
1 *tablespoon chopped capers*
½ *cup chopped celery*

1 *grated, peeled carrot*
2 *tablespoons lemon juice*
¼ *cup mayonnaise*
½ *teaspoon salt*
pepper to taste

Mix ingredients thoroughly, and refrigerate until ready to serve.

Makes 6 sandwiches or salad for 4 to 6.

SHRIMP SALAD

1 *pound cooked, chopped shrimp*
1 *cup chopped celery*
2 *tablespoons pickle relish, drained*
4 *scallions, sliced*
½ *cup mayonnaise*
½ *teaspoon salt*
pepper to taste

Combine ingredients, and chill.

Makes 6 sandwiches.

COFFEE SHOP HAM SALAD

Served with a few radishes and olives and potato chips, this is a tasty meal.

1 *pound boiled ham, minced*
½ *cup minced red onion*
½ *cup minced sweet pickles*
1 *cup chopped celery*
2 *hard-boiled eggs, chopped fine*
½ *cup mayonnaise*
1 *tablespoon prepared mustard*

Mix ingredients well, and refrigerate for at least 1 hour.

Makes 6 good-sized sandwiches on buttered toasted white bread, or a luncheon salad for 4.

CHRISTMAS SALAD

3½ *cups cooked, cubed, turkey breast*
1½ *cups finely chopped celery*
 ½ *cup chopped tomatoes*
 ½ *cup crumbled crisp bacon*
 ½ *cup chopped pecans*
 ⅔ *cup mayonnaise*
 1 *teaspoon lemon juice*
   salt and pepper to taste

Combine turkey, celery, tomatoes, bacon, and pecans. Blend lemon juice into mayonnaise and stir into mixture. Season to taste. Serve on buttered toasted French bread.

Serves 6 to 8.

International Flavors in Salads

In one form or another, salads are eaten throughout the world. They vary from the soothing coolness of Raita, an Indian salad, to the exotic flavor of Lotus Root Salad, of Oriental origin, to a heartier French salad such as Salade Niçoise, and the Basque Tomato Salad, reminiscent of Spanish and French foods.

The salads in this chapter are adapted to American tastes and ingredients. They are intentionally not authentic, but are meant to capture the flavor of other cuisines.

SALADE NIÇOISE

A traditional French salad that makes a refreshing supper.

  1 *large head romaine lettuce*
 ½ *pound cooked green beans, cut into 1-inch lengths*
  1 *cucumber, peeled and sliced*
  2 *tomatoes, cut into wedges*
  1 *green pepper, cleaned and cut into thin strips*
  2 *cups sliced, boiled potatoes*
  2 *cans tuna, 7-ounce size, drained*
  2 *hard-boiled eggs, quartered*
  8 *pitted black olives*
  1 *teaspoon capers*
  6 *anchovies, drained and chopped*
 ⅔ *cup Vinaigrette Dressing (see index)*
 ½ *teaspoon fresh, chopped parsley*

Wash romaine lettuce, and pat dry. Tear into pieces, and cover the bottom of a wide salad or serving bowl. Arrange green beans, cucumber, tomatoes, green pepper, potato slices, and tuna in attractive sections over romaine lettuce. Garnish with hard-boiled eggs, black olives, capers, and anchovies. Add parsley to Vinaigrette Dressing. Bring the salad bowl to the table for viewing, then toss salad with Vinaigrette Dressing. Serve with toasted garlic bread.

Serves 4 to 6.

ANDALUSIAN SALAD

This salad is especially delicious for supper served with sliced chorizo (Spanish sausage), crusty Italian bread, and red wine.

  2 *tomatoes, peeled and cut into thin wedges*
  2 *red peppers, seeded and cut into julienne strips*
  2 *cups cooked rice, cooled*
  1 *small onion, minced*
  1 *clove garlic, crushed*
 ⅓ *cup vegetable oil*
  2 *tablespoons red wine vinegar*
    salt and pepper to taste

Combine ingredients and chill well.

Serves 4 to 6.

MEXICAN FIESTA SALAD

  1 *avocado, pitted, peeled, and cubed*
  2 *tablespoons lemon juice*
  1 *small head iceberg lettuce, torn into small pieces*
  2 *scallions, sliced*
 ½ *green pepper, chopped*
  1 *tomato, chopped*
  2 *ounces cheddar cheese*
 ¼ *cup olive oil*
 ¼ *teaspoon sugar*
 ¼ *teaspoon chili powder*
    salt and pepper to taste

Sprinkle 1 tablespoon lemon juice on avocado cubes, and toss. Place in a bowl, and add lettuce, scallions, green pepper, tomato, and cheddar cheese. Combine. In a small bowl, put remaining lemon juice, olive oil, sugar, chili powder, and salt and pepper to taste. Beat vigorously; pour over salad, and toss.

Serves 4.

GREEK SALAD

   1 *head romaine lettuce*
   2 *ripe medium-sized tomatoes, cut into wedges*
   1 *green pepper, chopped*
   2 *scallions, sliced*
   8 *black olives (use Greek olives if available)*
   1 *cup marinated artichoke hearts*
   1 *small cucumber, diced*
   ½ *pound feta cheese*
   ½ *cup olive oil*
   1 *lemon*
   1 *tablespoon red wine vinegar*
   1 *clove garlic, crushed*
   ¼ *teaspoon dried oregano*
   ½ *teaspoon salt*
     fresh ground pepper to taste

Tear lettuce into small pieces, and place it in a salad bowl with the tomatoes, green pepper, scallions, black olives, artichoke hearts, and cucumber. Crumble cheese and sprinkle over salad. In a separate bowl, whisk together remaining ingredients, and pour over salad. Toss and serve immediately.

Serves 6.

BASQUE TOMATO SALAD

Try this with cold cuts, toasted French bread and red wine. The Basques are a nomadic people who roam the western edge of the Pyrenees. Their cooking has Spanish and French overtones.

   3 *large ripe tomatoes, peeled and cut into strips*
   2 *red peppers, cleaned and cut into thin strips*
   1 *medium-sized, red onion, sliced very thin*
   ½ *cup olive oil*
   2 *tablespoons red wine vinegar*
   ½ *teaspoon paprika*
   1 *small clove garlic, crushed*
   ½ *teaspoon salt*
   ½ *teaspoon fresh ground pepper*

Place tomatoes, red peppers, and onion in a bowl. Combine remaining ingredients, and pour over tomatoes. Cover, and chill thoroughly.

Serves 6.

ITALIAN ANTIPASTO SALAD

Traditionally an appetizer, this salad dish can be expanded to a light supper.

> 1 *can artichoke hearts, 14-ounce size, drained*
> 1 *cup cubed salami*
> 1 *cup cubed mozzarella cheese*
> 2 *hard-boiled eggs, chopped*
> 1 *tomato, cut into wedges*
> 1 *tablespoon capers*
> 2 *tablespoons chopped green pepper*
> 1 *small onion, cut into rings*
> 4 *anchovies, chopped*
> ½ *cup Italian Dressing (see index)*

Combine ingredients thoroughly, but gently.

Serves 4.

RAITA

Of Indian origin, this is a lovely side dish or condiment with a curry entrée.

> 1 *large cucumber*
> *salt*
> 2 *tablespoons grated green pepper*
> 1 *cup plain yogurt*
> ½ *teaspoon sugar*
> *fresh ground pepper*

Peel cucumber, grate, and sprinkle with salt. Cover and refrigerate for 30 minutes. Drain thoroughly. Combine with remaining ingredients.

Serves 4.

SCANDINAVIAN MUSHROOM SALAD

This is a delicious appetizer or accompaniment to a main dish.

    ½ pound fresh mushrooms, quartered
    1 tablespoon lemon juice
    1 tablespoon dry sherry
    1 tablespoon grated onion
    ⅓ cup heavy cream
      salt and pepper to taste

Place mushrooms in ½-inch boiling water, cover, and cook for 2 minutes. Drain in colander. In a bowl, combine lemon juice, sherry, onion, and heavy cream with mushrooms, and season with salt and pepper.

Serves 4.

LOTUS ROOT SALAD

If you have never eaten lotus root, prepare for a very different treat. Perhaps without knowing it, you may have sampled lotus root in Chinese dishes. It can be purchased in most Oriental markets.

    1 pound lotus root
    1 tablespoon lemon juice
    2½ cups cold water
    2½ cups boiling water
    2 tablespoons sesame oil
    1 tablespoon soy sauce
    1 tablespoon sugar
    ½ teaspoon salt

Wash lotus root and peel it. Cut into ⅛-inch thick slices, and drop into 2½ cups cold water with 1 tablespoon lemon juice. Transfer lotus root to 2½ cups boiling water, and cook for 3 or 4 minutes. Drain. Blend remaining ingredients, and pour over lotus root slices. Cover and chill for 1 hour.

Serves 4 to 6.

ORIENTAL CHICKEN SALAD
WITH SNOW PEA PODS

2 *chicken breasts, cooked, skinned and boned*
1 *package, 10-ounce size, frozen pea pods, cooked and drained*
½ *cup chopped water chestnuts*
3 *scallions, sliced thin*
½ *cup mayonnaise*
2 *teaspoons soy sauce*
1 *teaspoon sesame oil*
1 *teaspoon lemon juice*

Chop chicken breasts into cubes, and put into a bowl with the cooked snow pea pods, water chestnuts, and scallions. In a separate bowl, blend together mayonnaise, soy sauce, sesame oil, and lemon juice. Pour over chicken mixture and toss. Chill thoroughly.

Serves 4.

MEDITERRANEAN SARDINE SALAD

This highly seasoned salad combines all the best flavors of the Mediterranean.

8 *ounces macaroni shells*
2 *tomatoes, peeled and chopped*
½ *cup pitted black olive halves*
1 *small red onion, chopped*
½ *cup chopped green pepper*
¼ *cup fresh chopped parsley*
½ *cup olive oil*
2 *tablespoons red wine vinegar*
½ *teaspoon dry mustard*
½ *teaspoon dried thyme*
½ *teaspoon dried basil*
1 *teaspoon salt*
  fresh ground pepper to taste
2 *cans boneless, skinless sardines, 4¾ -ounce size, drained*

Cook macaroni according to package directions, and drain. Place in a large bowl, and combine with tomatoes, black olives, onion, green pepper and parsley. In a small bowl, blend olive oil, vinegar, mustard, thyme, basil, salt and pepper. Pour over salad, and toss until ingredients are well coated with dressing. Refrigerate for several hours. Just before serving, toss in sardines.

Serves 6.

WEINGELEE

1 *package gelatin*
1 *cup water*
1 *tablespoon lemon juice*
4 *tablespoons sugar*
1 *cup dry white wine*
½ *cup sliced strawberries*
½ *cup sliced peaches*
½ *cup pitted cherries*

Put ½ cup of water into a small saucepan, and add gelatin. Soak for a few minutes, and heat over a low flame, stirring until gelatin dissolves. Stir in lemon juice and sugar. Continue stirring until sugar melts. Remove from heat. Add remaining ½ cup water and wine. Chill until syrupy, then add fruit and spoon into a 1-quart mold. Chill thoroughly.

Serves 4 to 6.

SALADE INCA

1½ *pounds jumbo shrimp, peeled, deveined, and cooked*
1 *stalk celery, sliced very thin*
1 *teaspoon lemon juice*
1 *teaspoon fresh chopped parsley*
½ *cup Thousand Island Dressing (see index)*

Place shrimp and celery in a salad bowl. Sprinkle with lemon juice. Blend in dressing; sprinkle parsley over top. Chill thoroughly before serving.

Serves 4.

SALADE A LA CAFE DE PARIS

I had this delicious salad at the busy Cafe de Paris on Rome's Via Veneto. This cheerful restaurant is famous for its salad bar, where salads are prepared freshly each morning.

> 1 *can white cannellini beans, 20-ounce size, drained*
> 2 *stalks celery, chopped*
> 1 *small green pepper, chopped*
> 1 *small head iceberg lettuce, shredded*
> 1 *medium-sized tomato, chopped*
> 2 *shredded carrots*
> ½ *cup Italian Dressing (see index)*

Combine beans, celery, green pepper, lettuce, tomato, and carrots. Pour dressing over and toss gently to mix.

Serves 6.

SWEDISH RED CABBAGE AND APPLE SALAD

> 2 *tablespoons bacon drippings*
> 1 *tablespoon vegetable oil*
> 4 *cups finely shredded red cabbage*
> 3 *tart ripe apples, peeled, cored and sliced thin*
> 4 *tablespoons vinegar*
> 1 *tablespoon sugar*
> 2 *tablespoons orange juice*
>   *salt and pepper*

Heat bacon drippings and oil in a large pan. Add cabbage and apples. Barely cover with hot water, and bring to a boil. Reduce heat to a simmer and cook for about 15 minutes. Drain. Add vinegar, sugar, and orange juice to cabbage mixture. Season with salt and pepper. Serve hot or cold.

Serves 6.

Buffet Salads

Buffet salads are company dishes, although there is no reason why they cannot be eaten every day—it won't spoil the palate too much. As they are often served on large platters, you cannot do too much to garnish a buffet salad. They should be fresh and colorful, and should look almost too tasty to eat.

A delightful buffet salad that takes the burden off a busy host or hostess is a bowl of crisp greens surrounded by smaller bowls of vegetables and dressings. Each guest is expected to improvise a salad to his or her liking.

You can also surround a platter of greens with an assortment of foods: vegetables (raw or cooked), cold meat, fish (raw or cooked), cheese, and fruits. Serve a vinaigrette and a creamy fruit dressing on the side. With crusty French bread and a good wine, it is a complete meal.

The recipes in this section should start you thinking about the possibilities for entertaining large groups with salads.

CRUNCHY FISH SALAD

This is the salad pictured on the cover.

2 *pounds haddock, or other fish fillets, fresh or frozen*
2 *cups boiling water*
2 *teaspoons salt*
1 *small onion, sliced*
⅓ *cup lemon juice*
¾ *cup commercial herb and garlic dressing*
½ *cup sliced green onions*
2 *cups sliced, cooked carrots*
2 *cups peeled, diced cucumbers*
2 *tablespoons diced pimiento*
2 *cups celery, sliced thin diagonally*
1 *cup sour cream*
¼ *cup horseradish*
1 *teaspoon dill weed*
⅛ *teaspoon white pepper*
   crisp salad greens
   cucumber or tomato, sliced (for garnish)

If using frozen fish, thaw in the refrigerator. Cut fillets into 1-inch pieces. Place pieces in 10-inch frying pan. Add water, 1 teaspoon salt, onion, and ¼ cup lemon juice. Cover and simmer 5 to 10 minutes or until fish flakes easily when tested with a fork. Carefully remove fish from liquid; drain, and place in a bowl. Add onions, carrots, cucumbers, celery, and pimiento; toss lightly. Pour half of the herb and garlic dressing over fish. Cover and chill 1 to 2 hours. Combine sour cream, horseradish, dill weed, pepper, and remaining lemon juice and 1 teaspoon salt. Mix well. Drain fish and vegetables; combine; fold in sour cream mixture gently. Serve on crisp salad greens. Garnish with cucumber and/or tomato slices.

Makes 8 to 10 servings.

TOMATO AND MOZZARELLA SALAD

4 *ripe tomatoes, sliced about ¼-inch thick*

8 *ounces mozzarella cheese, sliced into thin rounds*
½ *teaspoon dried basil*
½ *cup Basic French Dressing (see index)*

Arrange tomato slices and mozzarella rounds alternately on a shallow serving dish. Combine basil and dressing; pour over salad. Cover, and chill for 30 minutes.

Serves 6.

TURKEY SALAD WITH MANDARIN ORANGES

This is an excellent way to use leftover turkey.

4 *cups cubed, cooked turkey*
1 *small can mandarin oranges*
1 *cup chopped celery*
2 *tablespoons minced scallions*
⅔ *cup Vinaigrette Dressing (see index)*
  salt and pepper to taste
  lettuce (for garnish)

Place turkey, oranges, celery, and scallions in a large bowl. Pour on dressing; season to taste, and toss. Pile on lettuce greens in shallow serving dish.

Serves 6 to 8.

TOMATO AND ONION SALAD PLATTER

6 *tomatoes, sliced about ½ -inch thick*
1 *medium-sized red onion, sliced very thin*
⅔ *cup Basic French Dressing (see index)*
5 *hard-boiled eggs*
1 *teaspoon fresh, chopped parsley*
8 *anchovies*

Arrange tomatoes and onion slices alternately in shallow serving dish. (A round-shaped dish is particularly effective.) Pour dressing over top. Halve hard-boiled eggs and separate whites and yolks. Chop whites very fine, and make a 1-inch border with them around the tomatoes at the edge of the dish. Place the egg yolks in a large hand strainer. With the back of a spoon, force the yolks through the strainer, letting them fall over tomatoes in center of the dish. Sprinkle parsley over egg-yolk topping, and place rolled anchovies over the top of dish.

Serves 6 to 8.

Dressings

The marriage of salad and dressing is vital to successful saladmaking. Always add the dressing to the salad at the very last minute unless otherwise instructed. Before adding dressing, be sure salad greens and ingredients are as dry as possible so the dressing will coat them evenly. Use just enough dressing to coat salad ingredients. Extra dressing can always be added, but too much dressing will soak and spoil any salad. Remember there should be only a little extra dressing left in the bottom of the salad bowl. Although French and mayonnaise are most popular, there are hundreds of kinds of dressings. Other categories include cooked and uncooked dressings, sour cream dressings, and yogurt dressings.

There is nothing quite so good as a freshly made dressing — and they are really quite easy to make and far superior to bottled dressings. Prepare a pint of dressing at a time and store it in the refrigerator in a tightly closed jar. Simply shake well before using. Basic French Dressing, the key to all vinegar-and-oil type dressings, is made by mixing oil, vinegar or lemon juice, and salt and pepper. Dry mustard and herbs can be added as well as spices and chopped vegetables. The oil used can be corn, peanut, olive oil or vegetable oil, according to your tastes. The vinegar can be white or red, wine vinegar or cider vinegar. There are also delicious herb vinegars such as tarragon, basil and mint, all well worth experimenting with.

Many of the dressings in this book are made with mayonnaise. Mayonnaise dressings are heavier and thicker than vinegar and oil, and should be used on heartier salads with meat, pastas, potatoes and eggs. There is no better base for these cream dressings than your own mayonnaise.

BASIC FRENCH DRESSING

Every French cook has a variation of this basic dressing. It is always a simple vinegar-and-oil mixture, rather than the heavy orange topping that is erroneously called French Dressing. This vinaigrette is the perfect dressing for any green salad, and in the variations listed below, it will complement a great variety of other salads.

> ¾ cup vegetable oil
> ¼ cup wine vinegar
> ½ teaspoon dry mustard
> ½ teaspoon salt
> freshly ground pepper to taste

Beat ingredients together with a wire whisk. Chill, and beat vigorously or shake well in a jar with a tight-fitting lid before using.

Makes approximately 1 cup.

Variations

Anchovy: Add 4 anchovy fillets, crushed into paste, to 1 cup Basic French Dressing.

Blue Cheese: Add 2 tablespoons crumbled blue cheese to 1 cup Basic French Dressing.

Caper: Add 2 tablespoons chopped capers to 1 cup Basic French Dressing.

Garlic: Add 2 cloves garlic, crushed, to 1 cup Basic French Dressing.

Italian: Add 1 clove garlic and ½ teaspoon oregano to 1 cup Basic French Dressing. Strain (optional).

Mustard: Add 1 teaspoon prepared mustard to 1 cup Basic French Dressing.

Roquefort: Add 2 tablespoons crumbled Roquefort cheese to 1 cup Basic French Dressing.

Vinaigrette: Add ½ teaspoon dried tarragon, ½ teaspoon dried chives, and 1 tablespoon finely chopped shallots to 1 cup Basic French Dressing.

Fines Herbes: Add ½ teaspoon dried tarragon, ½ teaspoon dried chives, ½ teaspoon chervil to 1 cup Basic French Dressing.

CURRY DRESSING

> ½ cup olive oil
> 2 tablespoons lemon juice
> 1 small onion, finely chopped
> 1 clove garlic, crushed
> 1 teaspoon curry powder
>   salt and pepper to taste

Beat ingredients with a wire whisk until mixed.

Makes a little over ½ cup.

LIME FRENCH DRESSING

> ½ cup vegetable or olive oil
> 3 tablespoons lime juice
> 1 tablespoon grated red onion
> ½ teaspoon grated lime rind
>   salt and pepper to taste

Using a wire whisk, combine ingredients thoroughly.

Makes about ¾ cup.

SOUR CREAM DRESSING

Try this on potato and pasta salads.

> 1 cup sour cream
> 1 tablespoon lemon juice

> 1 *tablespoon grated onion*
> ½ *teaspoon horseradish*
> ½ *teaspoon salt*
> ½ *teaspoon sugar*
> 1 *teaspoon dried parsley*
> *dash Tabasco sauce*

Combine ingredients, and chill.

Makes about 1½ cups.

CURRY AND SOUR CREAM DRESSING

This is especially good on chicken and meat salads.

> ¼ *cup sour cream*
> ¼ *cup mayonnaise*
> 1 *teaspoon lemon juice*
> ½ *teaspoon grated onion*
> 1 *teaspoon finely chopped parsley*
> 1 *teaspoon chopped chives*
> ¼ *teaspoon curry powder*
> ½ *teaspoon soy sauce*
> *salt and pepper to taste*

Combine ingredients thoroughly; chill for 30 minutes before using.

Makes about ½ cup.

MAYONNAISE

Homemade mayonnaise frightens many cooks unnecessarily. Not only is it easy to make, but once you have tried it, you won't want to use anything else. The secret to successful mayonnaise is to bring all the ingredients to room temperature before starting. Mayonnaise-based dressings are perfect with meat, poultry, and other hearty salads.

2 *egg yolks*
½ *teaspoon salt*
1 *teaspoon dry mustard*
2 *good dashes cayenne pepper*
¼ *cup vinegar*
2 *cups vegetable oil*
   or
1 *cup each vegetable and olive oil*

Place egg yolks in a deep bowl, and beat with a wire whisk until thickened and lemon yellow. Add salt, dry mustard, cayenne pepper, and half of the vinegar. Combine well. Add oil to the mixture, *drop by drop*, constantly beating with a whisk or electric mixer. As the mixture begins to thicken, add increasingly larger quantities of oil until all has been used. Drizzle in the remaining vinegar, beating constantly. Chill thoroughly.

Note: If you have added the oil too quickly into the egg yolks, the mixture may separate. To remedy, beat 1 egg yolk and add to the mayonnaise a bit at a time, beating constantly.

Makes about 2 cups.

HERBED MAYONNAISE DRESSING

½ *cup mayonnaise, preferably homemade*
1 *tablespoon wine vinegar*
1 *teaspoon chopped fresh parsley*
   or
½ *teaspoon dried parsley*
½ *teaspoon dried tarragon*
½ *teaspoon chopped fresh or frozen chives*
1 *scallion, finely sliced*

Combine ingredients, and chill thoroughly.

Makes a little over ½ cup.

CAPER MAYONNAISE

½ cup mayonnaise, preferably homemade
1 tablespoon chopped capers
1 teaspoon caper liquid
  dash curry powder

Combine ingredients, and chill thoroughly.

Makes about ½ cup.

GREEN GODDESS DRESSING

Add a drop of green food coloring to this dressing for a very nice touch.

1 cup mayonnaise, preferably homemade
1 tablespoon anchovy paste
  or
2 crushed anchovies
1 tablespoon finely chopped fresh parsley
1 clove garlic, crushed
¼ cup minced scallions
2½ tablespoons vinegar
1 teaspoon dried tarragon

Mix ingredients well, and chill for several hours before using.

Makes about 1½ cups.

THOUSAND ISLAND DRESSING

A traditional treat for a hearty tossed salad.

1 cup mayonnaise, preferably homemade
⅓ cup chili sauce
2 tablespoons chopped sweet pickles
1 teaspoon pickle juice
1 tablespoon chopped, stuffed green olives (optional)

Blend ingredients, and chill.

Makes about 1½ cups.

HONEY AND LIME DRESSING

⅓ cup honey
⅓ cup vegetable oil
⅓ cup lime juice
2 teaspoons grated lime rind

Combine ingredients well.

Makes about 1 cup.

FRUIT SALAD DRESSING

½ cup mayonnaise, preferably homemade
1 tablespoon lemon juice
1 tablespoon frozen orange juice concentrate
½ cup heavy cream, whipped

Combine mayonnaise, lemon juice, and orange juice. Fold in whipped cream.

Makes about 1 cup.

SPICY RUSSIAN DRESSING

1 cup mayonnaise, preferably homemade
¼ cup chili sauce
¼ cup finely chopped green pepper
¼ cup finely chopped pimiento
¼ cup finely chopped celery
1 tablespoon grated onion
dash Tabasco sauce

Combine ingredients, and chill for 30 minutes before using.

Makes about 2 cups.

DIET DRESSING

½ cup tomato juice
2 scallions, minced

1 *teaspoon chopped fresh parsley*
1 *tablespoon lemon juice*
½ *teaspoon Worcestershire sauce*
dash Tabasco sauce
¼ *teaspoon salt*
pepper to taste

Combine ingredients, and chill thoroughly. Mix before using by shaking vigorously in a covered jar.

Makes about ¾ cup.

COTTAGE CHEESE DRESSING

½ *cup cottage cheese*
¼ *cup skim milk*
1 *tablespoon chopped green pepper*
2 *tablespoons vinegar*
1 *teaspoon sugar*
salt and pepper to taste

Place ingredients in a blender, puréeing until smooth. Or, force cottage cheese through a sieve, and blend with other ingredients. Check seasoning.

Makes about 1 cup.

SLIMMER'S COTTAGE CHEESE DRESSING

1 *cup cottage cheese*
½ *cup buttermilk*
1 *tablespoon lemon juice*
1 *small clove garlic, crushed*
1 *tablespoon chopped olives*
¼ *teaspoon salt*
dash Tabasco sauce

Place ingredients in blender, and purée.

Makes about 1½ cups.

DIET HERB DRESSING

  1 *can tomato sauce, 8-ounce size*
  1 *tablespoon grated onion*
  1 *tablespoon lemon juice*
  1 *teaspoon Worcestershire sauce*
  ¼ *teaspoon dried basil*
  ¼ *teaspoon dried tarragon*
  ¼ *teaspoon celery seed*
  ½ *teaspoon salt*
    pepper to taste

Combine ingredients, and shake in tightly closed jar until well blended.

Makes a little over 1 cup.

LOW-CALORIE TOMATO DRESSING

  1 *cup tomato juice*
  2 *tablespoons red wine vinegar*
  1 *clove garlic, crushed*
  ¼ *teaspoon dry mustard*
  ¼ *teaspoon salt*
  ¼ *teaspoon dried basil*
  ¼ *teaspoon dried chervil*
    freshly ground pepper

Beat ingredients together; cover and chill. Shake or beat well before using.

Makes a little over 1 cup.

YOGURT DRESSING

This dressing is delicious on crisp lettuce greens and cucumbers.

  1 *cup plain yogurt*
  1 *teaspoon lemon juice*
  1 *clove garlic, crushed*

1 *teaspoon chopped chives*
½ *teaspoon dry mustard*
½ *teaspoon salt*
pepper to taste

Combine ingredients, and chill thoroughly.

Makes about 1 cup.

HERB-YOGURT DRESSING

1 *cup plain yogurt*
2 *tablespoons mayonnaise*
3 *scallions, thinly sliced*
2 *tablespoons finely chopped parsley*
2 *tablespoons finely chopped celery*
1 *tablespoon lemon juice*
1 *tablespoon horseradish*
1 *teaspoon sugar*
salt and pepper to taste

Combine ingredients in a bowl, and beat for 10 seconds. Adjust seasoning to taste.

Makes a little over 1½ cups.

FRUIT JUICE DRESSING

½ *cup grapefruit juice*
½ *cup orange juice*
1 *tablespoon vegetable oil*
1 *teaspoon lemon juice*
¼ *teaspoon dry mustard*
½ *teaspoon salt*
½ *teaspoon sugar*

Combine ingredients, and chill thoroughly. Shake well before using.

Makes about 1 cup.

EGG DRESSING

This dressing is a good complement to a salad of greens.

½ cup vegetable oil
2 tablespoons red wine vinegar
¼ teaspoon dry mustard
½ teaspoon salt
fresh ground pepper to taste
2 hard-boiled eggs, separated

Place oil, vinegar, mustard, salt and pepper in a bowl, and beat with a wire whisk. Force egg yolks through a sieve, and mix with dressing. Finely chop egg whites, and add to salad as garnish.

Makes about ¾ cup dressing.

LORENZO DRESSING

½ cup Basic French Dressing (see index)
⅓ cup chili sauce
¼ cup chopped watercress

Combine ingredients thoroughly, and chill well.

Makes about ¾ cup.

ORANGE MAYONNAISE

This dressing is delicious on fruit salad.

½ cup mayonnaise, preferably homemade
1 tablespoon concentrated, frozen orange juice
1 teaspoon grated orange rind

Combine ingredients, and chill.

Makes about ½ cup.

POPPY SEED DRESSING

½ cup vegetable oil
2 tablespoons wine vinegar
1 tablespoon prepared mustard
2 tablespoons poppy seeds
1 tablespoon honey
¼ teaspoon salt

Place all ingredients in an electric blender, and blend. Pour over salad, and serve immediately.

Makes about ¾ cup.

LEMON DRESSING

Try this on Bibb or Boston lettuce.

⅓ cup vegetable oil
1 tablespoon lemon juice
2 tablespoons heavy cream
½ teaspoon sugar
½ teaspoon salt
1 teaspoon grated lemon rind

Beat ingredients with wire whisk.

Makes about ½ cup.

CREAMY TARRAGON DRESSING

This dressing complements fish salads.

⅓ cup mayonnaise, preferably homemade
2 tablespoons tarragon vinegar
2 tablespoons heavy cream
pinch sugar

Whisk together ingredients, and chill for half an hour before serving.

Makes about ½ cup.

SESAME DRESSING

1 *cup plain yogurt*
¼ *cup toasted sesame seeds*
1 *tablespoon soy sauce*
1 *teaspoon lemon juice*
3 *tablespoons chopped scallions*
  pinch sugar
  salt and pepper to taste

Combine ingredients. Chill well.

Makes 1½ cups.

BUTTERMILK AND HERB DRESSING

This dressing will keep in tightly covered jar in refrigerator for several weeks.

1 *cup buttermilk*
1 *cup mayonnaise, preferably homemade*
½ *teaspoon garlic salt*
½ *teaspoon onion salt*
½ *teaspoon dried chives*
½ *teaspoon dried basil*
½ *teaspoon dried parsley*
½ *teaspoon paprika*
½ *teaspoon celery salt*
1 *tablespoon soy sauce*

Beat ingredients with wire whisk. Chill for 24 hours before serving.

Makes a little over 2 cups.

Herb Chart

Using herbs makes it possible to add special flavor to salads without great expense. Often the use of a particular herb can be the cause for a salad's success.

It is interesting to experiment with different herbs. Many can be grown in your own garden or potted and placed in a sunny window. In this way, you will always have your own supply of fresh herbs.

Fresh herbs are always best for full flavor, but dried herbs can be used with excellent results. It is possible to detect the age of dried herbs by smell and color. The greener the herb, the fresher it is likely to be, and the stronger the odor, the younger it is.

Do not store herbs near light or heat, because they are quickly robbed of their color and flavor. The best way to keep dried herbs is in individual, opaque containers with tight fitting lids. Store them in a cool place. Remember that dried herbs are stronger than fresh ones, so use less. Use about one-half as many dried herbs as fresh. Fresh herbs can be frozen in a plastic bag for a reasonable length of time. They will discolor slightly, but the flavor will remain quite good.

HERB CHART FOR SALADS

basil (sweet basil) A fragrant herb with full green leaves. It is particularly well suited to tomatoes, cucumbers, and seafood salads, but complements many other salads as well. Fresh, chopped basil is superb, and grows easily in a windowsill pot or garden where there is plenty of sun.

chervil An aromatic herb of the parsley family that, unfortunately, is little known in this country. Excellent in tossed salads, it is always used in French *fines herbes* combinations.

chives Delicately flavored greens of the onion family. They can be found fresh, frozen, or freeze-dried. They are fairly easy to grow in pots in a kitchen window, and worth the effort, for they add freshness to many salads.

dill An herb of the parsley family that is widely used in Scandinavia, Europe, and America. The leaves are called dill weed and are delicious when added to salads, especially those made with seafood and cucumber. Dill seed is used to season vinegar and vegetables. Fresh dill weed is often available in supermarkets.

garlic A relative of the onion family with a flavor that is quite strong and distinctive, garlic should always be used with a light touch. Garlic is a bulb, which is separated into cloves. The cloves should be peeled before using.

mint An aromatic herb of the mint plant family that has many varities. Fresh chopped mint is delicious in fruit salads, and adds an unusual flavor to green salads. It is easily grown.

mustard Made from crushed dried seeds of certain species of the mustard plant, mustard is essential in making a fine French dressing.

parsley A very popular herb for use in salad or as a garnish. Of course, it is best fresh, when it has a pungent flavor. Never leave it on a plate when used as a garnish because it is delicious and filled with vitamins.

rosemary An evergreen that adds an unusual touch to salads or salad dressings, rosemary is quite strong, and must be used with discretion.

tarragon One of the French *fines herbes,* tarragon has a distinct flavor with a slightly anise taste. Superb in salads and dressings, it is used to prepare flavored vinegar.

Salads are a joy in all seasons, although too many people tend to associate them with spring and summer meals when vegetables are most plentiful. This is an unfortunate assumption, because the variety of salads that do not depend on fresh seasonal vegetables and lettuce greens is virtually limitless. To provide inspiration for "salad meals," here are some menus for meals consisting of salads, made with ingredients that are available all year long. Some type of bread always complements salads well, along with another side dish, beverage, and dessert, if you have a sweet tooth. Introduce your family to new salads, and they will be delighted.

Luncheon Menus

Spinach, Mushroom and Bacon Salad
French Rolls
Pecan Pie
Iced Tea

Pea and Cheese Salad
Boiled Ham Rolls
Buttered Toast Rounds
Homemade Chocolate Chip Cookies
Coffee

Tomato Aspic with Chicken
Cucumber and Carrot Sticks with Curry Mayonnaise
Toasted French Bread
Lemon Sherbet
White Wine

143

Zesty Tuna and Egg Salad Sandwiches
Potato Chips
Pickles and Olives
Fresh Donuts
Milk

Tomato and Onion Salad Platter
Pumpernickel Rolls
Coffee Ice Cream
White Wine

Summer Fruit Salad
Finger Ham Sandwiches
Butter Cookies
Lemonade

Bean and Tuna Salad
Cranberry Sauce
Italian Bread
Vanilla Ice Cream with Toasted Almond Slivers
Iced Coffee

Lentil Salad
Serbian Salad
Corn Bread
Lime Pie
Red Wine

Romaine Salad
Hot Biscuits
Fruit and Cookies
White Wine

Butter Bean and Corn Salad
Broiled Hamburgers
Sautéed Tomatoes
Toasted French Bread
Hot Apple Pie with Whipped Cream
Red Wine

Swedish Red Cabbage and Apple Salad
Cold Cuts and Various Cheeses
Rye Bread and Butter
Banana Cake
Red Wine

Dinner Menus

Caesar Salad
Hot Garlic Bread
Chocolate Fudge Cake
White Wine

Tomatoes Stuffed with Rice and Shrimp
Green Salad I
Crackers
Raspberry Sherbet
Iced Tea

Crabmeat Salad Mold
Hot Asparagus
Crescent Rolls
Pecan Cookies and Vanilla Ice Cream
White Wine

Hot German Potato Salad
Boiled All-Beef Knockwurst
Seeded Rye Bread and Mustard
Hot Apple Turnover
Beer or Ale

Fanelli Salad
Sesame Rolls and Sweet Butter
German Chocolate Cake
Red Wine

Roast Beef and Potato Salad
Sliced Tomatoes with Fresh Ground Pepper
Toasted French Bread
Crème Caramel
Red Wine

Creamy Chicken Tarragon Salad
French Bread and Butter
Fresh Pears and Ripe Brie
White Wine

Nancy Dussault's Corned Beef Salad
Broccoli Spears
Hot Rolls
Nut and Date Cake
Red Wine

Cold Ziti Salad
Toasted Garlic Bread
Baked Cinnamon Apple
Red Wine

Swiss Cheese Salad
Cold, Sliced Roast Beef
Whole Wheat Rolls and Mustard
Fresh Pumpkin Pie
Red Wine

Index